LANDMINES
IN WAR AND PEACE

LANDMINES
IN WAR AND PEACE

MIKE CROLL

Pen & Sword
MILITARY

First published in Great Britain in 2008
By Pen and Sword Military
an imprint of
Pen and Sword Books Ltd
47 Church Street
Barnsley
South Yorkshire S70 2AS

ISBN 978 1 84415 841 6

A CIP record for this book is available from the British Library

Printed by the MPG Books Group
in the UK

Typeset by S L Menzies-Earl

Pen and Sword Books Ltd incorporates the imprints of
Pen and Sword Aviation, Pen and Sword Maritime, Pen and Sword Military,
Wharncliffe Local History, Pen and Sword Select,
Pen and Sword Military Classics and Leo Cooper.

For a complete list of Pen and Sword titles please contact
Pen and Sword Books Limited
47 Church Street, Barnsley, South Yorkshire, S70 2AS, England
E-mail: enquiries@pen-and-sword.co.uk
Website: www.pen-and-sword.co.uk

Contents

For Emma and Ben

Introduction

It is ten years since the signing of the mine ban treaty in Ottawa and coincidentally ten years since the publication of my book, *The History of Landmines*. This felt like an appropriate moment to consider the impact of the treaty, to review progress in humanitarian demining and to incorporate some aspects of the history that have come to light in recent years. I anticipated that I would simply write a few extra pages to bring the book up to date, but having started to unpick the first chapter, rather like a loose thread on a jumper, I continued pulling until the whole thing unravelled. Knitting it back together and incorporating all the new material was far harder and took far longer than I anticipated. So this is essentially a new book, not just refreshed but updated and rewritten.

I originally wrote *The History of Landmines* because I was interested in the subject, but it was remarkable how little had been written on the theme. Military history has rarely been fashionable, but in certain quarters it has long been popular. There are hundreds of books on military equipment – tanks, aircraft and guns – yet mines have always been neglected. They do not fire the imagination, they are far from heroic and the squat, drab-coloured tubs of explosive are hardly photogenic. Instead of illustrious names like Sherman, Spitfire or Kalashnikov, mines are known by a confusing collection of nomenclatures: OZM 72, M14, Mark 7.

The lack of interest in military aspects of mines is the result of a combination of factors. They are a defensive weapon and defensive battles are often under-reported. Their effectiveness is in part dependent on their concealment in the earth, but rather than giving them a secretive allure they are considered dull; agricultural rather than martial. They have an unnerving psychological effect first identified in the American Civil War when it was noted that 'Men will march bravely up through a blaze of musketry but will march timidly over ground in which they suspect the hidden mine.' Not only do soldiers dislike encountering mines, they take little pleasure in laying them, as articulated by Royal Engineer Colonel J.M. Lambert in 1952: 'Mine warfare is an unpleasant business. It is foreign to our character to kill a man a fortnight in arrears so to speak, when you yourself are out of harm's way; and most British soldiers who have experienced it will own a rooted dislike of mine warfare in principle and in practice.' In short, mines are boring and nasty.

Much has been written in recent years about the humanitarian mines issue. There is a significant corpus of survivor testimony, assessments of the impact of mines in the developing world, interminable consultants' papers and a great swathe of anti-mine literature, much of it highly emotive and not especially enlightening. In this book I aim to provide a concise, accessible overview of the mines issue from ancient times through to 2008, combining the military history and the modern humanitarian mines issue. It is a dispassionate account (an easy proposition for an Englishman) that provides context and an explanation of how mines came to proliferate. It is aimed at people wishing to gain an insight into the subject rather than at those who are professionally involved, although some of the latter may find new and interesting strands of information. I have tried to tell the story at pace, avoiding wearisome detail, but I fear my technical instincts may be apparent in places. I succeed, where others have failed, in finding the military history of mines absorbing.

It is a history with few personalities and fewer heroes, but it does take us around the world from central Gaul, to the cliffs of Malta, the banks of the Ohio, the sun-baked plains of Sudan, the mud of the Somme, the pebbly beaches of Southern England, the deserts of North Africa, the great European plain, the mountains of Korea, the jungles of Vietnam and the dirt roads of Africa. As well as place, technology is important to the story. Broadly, we can trace three major periods in the history of the mine, which we can concisely define as the victim-operated explosive trap. First, the wooden or metal spikes of the ancient world which were the antecedents of the modern mine, different in form, but identical in function. Second came gunpowder, used in various capricious forms for 500 years from China's Ming Dynasty through to the American Civil War. And third, high explosives that allowed the manufacture of small, powerful, reliable mines. The high-explosive mines developed through three generations: simple mines, some literally cake tins, that exploded when pressure was applied to the top; plastic mines with fuses that could resist clearance by rollers, flails or explosives; and finally scatterable mines, delivered by artillery or fast jet, with highly destructive warheads, target-discriminating fuses and self-neutralization facilities. The main driver for mine development has been the need to counter armoured attack, the lumbering Allied tanks of the First World War, the Nazi blitzkrieg of the Second World War and the threat of massed Soviet tanks in the Cold War.

Mines are not just another weapon that simply kills, they transform the terrain to a defender's advantage, channelling the enemy, allowing defenders to employ less men, whilst forcing an attacker to use more; they create fear and uncertainty beyond the casualties that they inflict and are an attritional weapon, wearing down an attackers' resources. They need to be part of an overall defensive plan and covered by fire if they are to be effective. And if carelessly laid, as they often have been, they can become a menace to friendly forces and a deadly plague to civilians.

In the late twentieth century the effects of careless minelaying became all too apparent with tens of thousands of people in the developing world becoming casualties of mines laid to protect them during interstate conflicts. 'We have a choice here,' a villager in Cambodia told me in 1992, 'mines around our village, or the Khmer Rouge in it.' Yet after the Khmer Rouge threat had gone, the mines remained and took an appalling toll on fragile communities emerging from decades of war. The sight of civilians losing their limbs to mines years after wars ended provoked a highly emotional and effective campaign to ban anti-personnel mines, the effects of which are becoming apparent, but they are not as clear cut as many campaigners may believe. The scale of the humanitarian mines crisis, whilst serious, was overstated by many. The UN estimate of 110 million mines buried world-wide turns out to be closer to 5 million. Demining efforts of the past twenty years, whilst undertaken by many very committed people, bear somewhat uncomfortable comparison with those in Europe after the Second World War when over 100 million mines (350,000 alone on the beaches of Southern England) were cleared in three years.

Ultimately, despite the tragedy of far too many civilian victims of mines, I predict that the end of mines is a very real prospect within a few years. In part this is because demining efforts are reducing the number of casualties and most buried mines could be cleared with a couple of years of concerted effort. But just as importantly, moral, circumstantial and technical factors will prevent many more mines being used in the future. The moral factor is the public revulsion at the indiscriminate effects of mines, the circumstantial is the ending of the armoured threat and with it the need for anti-tank minefields. The technical factor is the arrival of new forms of weapon that incorporate sophisticated surveillance systems which replace victim-operated mines.

Finally, a note of warning about figures relating to mines, be they relating to production, laying, clearing, casualties or cost. They are all contentious – 'Landmines, Damn Lies and Statistics' in the words of one deminer. Yet I found that figures were needed to illustrate the story and I have quoted many throughout the text. I have checked them using several sources, even so they should be regarded as indicative rather than gospel.

Chapter 1

The Beginning of Mines

—✄—

The foards are soon choakt up with calthorpes.
Francis Markham, 1622

In 52 BC Julius Caesar campaigned in Gaul to suppress an uprising against Roman domination. At a critical stage of the campaign the Gallic leader, Vercingetorix, withdrew his army of 80,000 to the fortified town of Alesia (near Dijon in Central France). Caesar deployed his army of 70,000 around the town intending to starve the Gauls into submission rather than risk attacking with his smaller force. However, on hearing that the Gauls were raising a large army to relieve their besieged compatriots, Caesar was faced with a dilemma: he could either retreat, abandoning Gaul; or he could attempt to maintain the siege whilst surrounded himself. Caesar chose to stand.

Inside Alesia, Vercingetorix had sufficient food for thirty days, forty if he reduced rations and expelled the women and children from the town, and asked the Romans to let them go. This he did, but Caesar, concerned about having to open a breach in his own fortifications, would not accept them and they were left to starve between the opposing armies. Meanwhile, the Gauls outside Alesia set about raising an army to lift the siege before Vercingetorix was starved out.

Caesar's situation was equally desperate. He faced the possibility of Vercingetorix sallying out of Alesia and a relieving force attacking his rear simultaneously. It is often said that the Romans won as many battles with the spade as with the sword and Caesar demonstrated how. He set about creating two lines of fortifications: the first a 16km long circumvallation[1] surrounding the town to prevent anyone escaping; and outside that, the second, a 21km long contravallation[2] to protect his troops from the relieving force. The Romans occupied the 650m wide strip of land between the two lines. The defences were not only extraordinarily long, but they were remarkably thorough, consisting of two trenches each 5m wide, in front of a palisade fence on top of an earth rampart, overlooked by stout wooden towers every 120m. The earth rampart was covered by a lattice of sharpened branches known as an abatis, with a further five rows of abatis in front of the trenches. In his *Commentaries on the Gallic War* Caesar described the rest of the defences:

> In front of them [the abatis], arranged in diagonal rows forming quincunxes, were pits three feet deep, tapering gradually towards the bottom, in which were imbedded smooth logs as thick as a man's thigh, with the ends sharpened and charred, and projecting only three inches above ground. To keep the logs firmly in position, earth was thrown into the pits and trodden down to a depth of one foot, the rest of the cavity being filled with twigs and brush wood to hide the trap. These were planted in groups, each containing eight rows three feet apart, and were nicknamed lilies from their resemblance to that flower. In front of these again were blocks of wood a foot long with iron hooks fixed in them, called goads by the soldiers. These were sunk right in the ground and strewn thickly everywhere.

The defences were completed in thirty days, just in time to meet the relieving Gallic force which Caesar claimed was 250,000 strong.[3] On the first day of the three–day battle Roman cavalry sallied out of the defences and defeated the relieving force's cavalry. The following day, under cover of darkness, the Gauls attempted to breach the Roman lines using spades, fascines,[4] grappling hooks and ladders. On hearing the assault, Vercingetorix led his men out of the town and into battle. There was a fierce exchange of arrows and stone missiles, but as the Gauls got close to the Roman lines they 'found themselves pierced by the goads or tumbled into the pits and impaled themselves, whilst others were killed by heavy siege spears discharged from the ramparts and towers ... and they failed to penetrate the defences at any point,' wrote Caesar. Again the frustrated Gauls withdrew to their camps.

On the third day there was fighting simultaneously all over the field. The Gauls heaped soil over the obstacles and attacked with shields locked above their heads, fresh troops continually relieving those who were tired. The hard-pressed Romans fought desperately, with Caesar redistributing his forces to meet each new attack. The decisive act was the deployment of the Roman cavalry who sallied out and appeared suddenly behind the attacking Gauls, who panicked and were mown down by the cavalry as they attempted to retreat. On seeing his countrymen in flight, Vercingetorix surrendered, bringing to an end Gallic resistance to Roman rule.

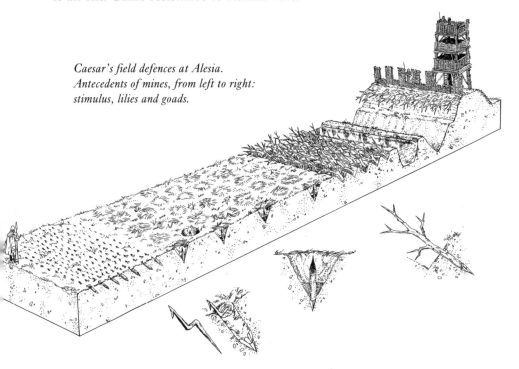

Caesar's field defences at Alesia.
Antecedents of mines, from left to right:
stimulus, lilies and goads.

This dramatic battle provides the best-recorded example of extensive early use of the antecedents of the modern mine. Goads and lilies were victim-operated traps, collectively forming an area-denial weapon, deployed to disrupt an attacking formation by hindering the occupation of, or the advance across, an area. The principles of their use have remained constant since the beginning of formal war making. They are weapons of defence deployed to deter, slow, unnerve and endanger an attacker. Like all defences, the stronger they are, the more troops are needed to overcome them, and conversely, the fewer defenders are needed.

To achieve an element of surprise, Caesar's goads were hidden in the grass and his lilies were covered by brushwood, in much the same as modern mines are concealed. They were laid in some depth to ensure that they could not be quickly crossed. The depth was roughly that of a strongly hurled spear, so any attempt to remove the traps would have to be done under 'fire'. It also meant that in order for the attackers to fire upon the defenders, they had to enter the 'minefield'. Covering minefields with fire remains a key requirement to ensure their effectiveness. Having a variety of traps demands that attackers employ a variety of breaching techniques – at Alesia this meant unearthing the goads, throwing baskets of soil to fill in the lilies and using ropes to pull out the abatis. This required time to prepare and effective choreography to ensure progress. Crossing the minefield canalized the attackers in the narrow lanes cleared by breaching teams. This made them vulnerable to enfilade fire whilst they were unable to effectively bring their own weapons to bear on the defenders. Finally, leaving safe lanes in a minefield allowed the defending side to sally forth and confront attackers which, as Caesar demonstrated, could be highly effective. A minefield is not a passive barrier, but if built into an overall defensive effort, it is a highly effective killing zone and is therefore a force multiplier, boosting defensive strength well beyond numerical strength.

Roman lilies have been located along the Antonine Wall in Scotland dating from the second century AD and were doubtless used to enhance fortifications elsewhere. Famously, lily pits were also used by the Scots at the Battle of Bannockburn in 1314 against superior English cavalry. Perhaps more surprisingly, lilies, or wolf hole as they also became known, were used by German troops in front of their trenches at Passchendaele in 1917.

Whilst undeniably effective, goads and lilies were somewhat inflexible and inefficient, taking a good deal of time to prepare and to dig in. The same function was more commonly provided by the more versatile caltrop (also called calthrop, crows' feet, murex, tetrahedron or tribulus).[5] This simple device had four short spikes fixed together so that when thrown on the ground three spikes formed a stable base with the fourth pointing upwards. Some had the spikes set in a wooden or resin ball, others had the spikes twisted and hammered together; more recent versions are riveted or welded. But the arrangement of the four spikes, and the overall dimensions of between 12 and 15cm across, have not changed since ancient times.[6]

Caltrops could rapidly be emplaced on a battlefield. They were soon concealed amongst grass or short vegetation and could easily penetrate the thin leather soles of sandals (or indeed thick rubber soles of modern combat boots) and pierce deep into a man's foot. The resulting debilitating wound would be susceptible to infection, with the victim left largely immobile for weeks or months. Horses, camels or elephants were equally vulnerable to injury, throwing their riders in the ensuing panic.

Caltrops were particularly effective against the tightly packed infantry formations of the ancient world which would rapidly lose their cohesion if soldiers were impaled by concealed caltrops, causing men to fall, creating gaps to be exploited by the opposing side. Alexander the Great's father, Philip of Macedon, used caltrops in his victory over the Athenians and Thebans in 338 BC. Alexander himself encountered caltrops used by Darius III at the Battle of Gaugamela in 331 BC, but was able to manoeuvre around them to defeat the Persians.

The Romans kept supplies of caltrops in forts to deploy against attackers and also used them in open warfare. The Roman General Macrinus campaigning against the Parthian Empire (centred on modern-day Iran) used caltrops to cover a withdrawal during the Battle of Nisibis in AD 217 as recorded by Herodian:

And when the size of the cavalry and the number of camels began to cause them [the Romans] trouble, they pretended to retreat and then threw down caltrops and other keen-edged iron devices. They were

A caltrop, typically about 12cm from tip to tip. When thrown on the ground, three points form a base with the third pointing upwards to inflict a painful and debilitating wound to a man or horse.

fatal to the cavalry and the camel riders as they lay hidden in the sand, and were not seen by them. The horses and the camels trod on them and fell onto their knees and were lamed, throwing the riders off their backs.

Publius Flavius Vegetius,[7] author of the Roman military manual 'De Re Militari', provided further evidence of their effectiveness: 'The Roman soldiers rendered [chariots] useless chiefly by the following contrivance: at the instant the engagement began, they strewed the field of battle with caltrops, and the horses that drew the chariots, running full speed on them, were infallibly destroyed.'[8]

Chariots were not the only ancient wheeled vehicles that were thwarted by the antecedents of landmines. Philo Mechanicus of Byzantium, writing in the second century BC described a victim-operated trap designed to stop heavy siege engines. These were large earthenware jars that were buried outside city walls and carefully concealed – soldiers could pass over them, but they would collapse under the weight of approaching siege engines.

After the classical age caltrops were incorporated into the armouries of most armies and were used extensively. At the Battle of Jalula in 637, the Persians defended their position against Muslim Arabs using extensive fields of caltrops. In 1213, China's Jin Dynasty temporarily halted the advance of Genghis Khan outside Zhongdu by surrounding the city with caltrops, according to some reports, for a distance of 50km. The English army used them in France, at Crècy in 1346, and to defend Orleans in 1429, where Joan of Arc was wounded by treading on one. Caltrops featured in some noble families' coats of arms, suggesting that their use was celebrated even in the age of chivalry. In Japan caltrops were known as tetsu-bishi and were used by Ninjas since the fourteenth century. During the Wars of the Roses in fifteenth-century England, the logical step was made of sewing nails onto long nets to create obstacles that could be deployed and repositioned rapidly. Sketches of caltrops appear in the notebooks of Leonardo da Vinci, who recommended that cavalry keep caltrops in leather satchels to scatter if pursued, and that horses be shod with iron plates to prevent them from being injured. Swedish crossbowmen in the sixteenth century used caltrops to defend against cavalry attacks, and the first settlers in Jamestown, Virginia, used them to defend against Indians in the seventeenth century. The British Army used them in the Crimea and Sudan in the nineteenth century, and stockpiled large quantities for use by Home Guard forces defending Britain during the Second World War. They appeared again on the battlefields of South-East Asia in the late twentieth century and remain in use in many armies today, linked by chains to form instant road blocks. With a lineage spanning three millennia, caltrops are the most enduring weapon system in existence and the direct descendants of the modern mine.

Notes

1 From Latin *circum*, around, and *vallum*, rampart.
2 A second line of fortifications behind the circumvallation facing away from the enemy position to protect the besiegers from external attacks.
3 Caesar's estimate is almost certainly an exaggeration. The real figure was probably less than half that, but even so he was greatly outnumbered by the Gauls.
4 A bundle of brushwood laid to help troops advance across a gap or marshy or uneven ground. They remain in use, normally transported by tanks for exactly the same purpose.
5 The etymology of caltrop may stem from the Latin calx, heel + *trippa*, trap, or from the spiky plant, the Star Thistle, or *Centaurea calcitrapa*.
6 Caltrops were used at least 250 years before Alesia. Why Caesar used the less versatile and more labour-intensive goads is unclear. It could be that, as they used half the iron of a caltrop, Caesar was making the best use of limited resources.
7 Vegetius is perhaps best known for the adage 'Si vis pacem para bellum', 'If you want peace, prepare for war'.
8 Apart from in Britain, the use of chariots on the battlefield peaked several centuries before the rise of the Roman Empire. Their effectiveness depended on level unbroken ground and this could be easily altered, not only by using caltrops, but by strewing boulders or digging shallow ditches on anticipated approach routes. Long after their effectiveness on the battlefield was undermined, the Romans enjoyed the spectacle of charioteering in the form of races in the Circus Maximus.

Chapter 2

Gunpowder Mines

—ᴍᴍ—

Neither a proper nor an effective method of war.
Confederate General James Longstreet

In the ninth century, the Chinese discovered a substance with magical powers: an explosion was produced when charcoal was burnt on soil with a high concentration of sulphur. For hundreds of years experiments were conducted which resulted in the production of what eventually became known as gunpowder, or black powder: a mixture of charcoal, sulphur and potassium nitrate, finely ground and mixed in roughly equal proportions.

Sulphur is found in many volcanic parts of the world and is easily recognized by its yellow colour and pungent smell. Charcoal, made by burning wood in the absence of air, is widely available. Potassium nitrate, or saltpetre, occurs in decomposing organic matter and can be produced by composting, leaching and drying an unsavoury mixture of faeces, urine and lime. Sulphur burns with a small blue flame and charcoal only smoulders. The key is potassium nitrate which provides oxygen, allowing the charcoal and sulphur to burn rapidly with a large increase in volume of hot gasses.

Gunpowder can easily be set off by a flame and in the open air, it simply burns quickly. But in a confined space the pressure will build up sufficiently to produce an explosion. It has a force that pushes rather than cuts, so it can heave a ball from a cannon, but it will not slice its breach. For 500 years, until the discovery of the much more powerful high explosives such as Dynamite, or TNT (explored in the next chapter), gunpowder was the main ingredient in warfare.[1]

Since the beginning of gunpowder attempts were made to incorporate it into mines. For all of its magical powers, it could only be used in dry conditions as it is hygroscopic – it absorbs water from the atmosphere – and therefore loses its explosive ability. Keeping out moisture, especially when emplaced underground, was a considerable challenge in the pre-plastic world. When Cromwell said, 'Put your faith in God and keep your powder dry,' he was being deadly serious.

Assuming gunpowder could be kept dry, setting it off was simple enough – just apply a match or spark. Muskets or cannons could be fired by the soldiers who operated them. But a mine, an explosive successor to the caltrop, needed a means of firing itself independently when activated by its victim. A reliable means of firing a victim-operated explosive trap was not developed until the mid-nineteenth century.

Gunpowder was first used on the battlefield in thirteenth-century China, initially in fireworks or simple bombs that might have impressed many but would have killed or injured few. But they went on to develop guns, rockets and various forms of mine notable for their ingenuity rather than for their contribution to winning battles. One of the earliest victim-operated devices was the Ming Dynasty's 'underground sky-soaring thunder' which consisted of a group of attractive objects – lances, pikes and flags – that were set in the ground to attract trophy hunting horsemen. The act of pulling a pole from the ground disturbed a bowl beneath the staffs which contained a slow-burning incandescent material, which in turn fired a gunpowder charge.

The fourteenth-century Chinese military treatise, the *Huolongjing*, describes early command-initiated fragmentation mines. Fragmentation was, and remains, a method of using explosive force to shatter (fragment) and project potentially lethal metal casing. The early Chinese versions were iron cannon balls filled with gunpowder, with a long fuse that was ignited by hand. More extraordinary is the description of one victim-operated fragmentation mine. This was made from a long piece of bamboo, waterproofed with oil and cowhide, filled with compressed gunpowder together with lead or iron pellets (fragmentation) and sealed with wax. The fuze was a clockwork mechanism with steel wheels rotated by a falling weight attached to a cord rotated about an axle. When an intruder stepped onto a disguised board, a pin was dislodged causing the weights to fall, turning the steel wheels against a flint, the resulting sparks firing the buried mine.

Gunpowder was discovered in Europe by the English Franciscan Friar, Roger Bacon,[2] towards the end of the thirteenth century, but the ingenious Chinese devices were not known to Europeans for many centuries after their invention. Initial European attempts to use gunpowder in mines focussed on a fragmentation device which became known as the fougasse.[3] Strictly speaking it was not a mine as it was neither victim operated nor mass produced. However, modern fragmentation mines were developed from the fougasse, so its history is entirely relevant.

The fougasse consisted of a cone-shaped hole dug in the ground, narrow end down, angled towards likely avenues of attack. A gunpowder charge was placed at the bottom of the hole which was then covered with rocks. When the charge was fired, the rocks were blown over a wide area. It was best suited to static defences where it had the potential to stop massed charges. The fougasse was, however, very much the poor man's artillery. It could not be redirected once emplaced or reloaded once fired, the hole would fill with water when it rained and it was difficult to fire the underground charge.

The best-preserved fougasse emplacements can still be found around Malta where they were integrated into the island's defences by the Knights of St John under the instruction of their resident military engineer, the Italian Francesco Maradon. By 1770, he had established a network of over sixty operational systems overlooking potential landing sites, although despite these, Napoleon's troops landed unopposed in 1798. Brigadier Lawson tested a Maltese fougasse in 1802, loading it with 64kg of gunpowder and ten tonnes of rocks. 'The explosion,' he wrote, 'resembled the tremendous discharge of a volcano.'

Late eighteenth-century military engineering treatises recommended the use of similar fragmentation devices around fixed fortifications. 'The burying of caissons [ammunition boxes] is also

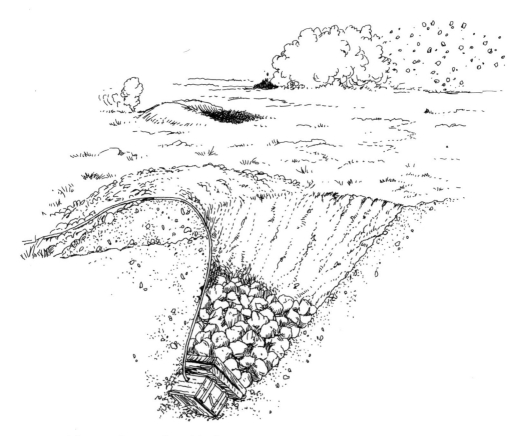

A fougasse, the antecedent of the fragmentation mine, was of capricious reliability.

productive of a good effect. These are small chests, 2 or 3 feet long and a foot and half broad, filled with powder. They are fired at any time by a [powder] train conveyed in a wooden trough in a covert way. Sometimes shells are put in these caissons then they produce still greater effect'[4]

Gunpowder's hygroscopic property also limited the effectiveness of these weapons as the fuse or the charge became damp and would not burn or explode. This could be mitigated to a degree by filling a cloth seam with gunpowder and proofing it with pitch in a narrow wooden trough. But firing a fougasse remained an uncertain process, with defenders unsure until the last moment if their device would work.

A solution appeared in 1831 in the unlikely form of a Methodist philanthropist called William Bickford.

Bickford was a leather merchant from the West of England, a region with many tin mines, gunpowder being used to blast rock to extract the tin. Bickford became concerned at the number of accidents to tin miners caused by handling gunpowder and had a flash of inspiration on how to ameliorate the situation when visiting a yarn–spinning factory. He designed a machine that tightly wound strands of jute around a central core of gunpowder which were then immersed in a bath of hot varnish and coated with chalk dust to prevent the fuse from sticking together. The result was impressively simple. His safety fuse had a consistent and predictable rate of burning (commonly 2ft a minute) – not only was it insulated from atmospheric moisture, it could be used underwater and was easily lit by application of a flame to one end. It was an immediate success, with 45 miles of fuse produced in Bickford's factory's first year of operation. Although designed by a philanthropist to prevent accidents in tin mines, safety fuse was soon incorporated for military use.[5]

With the introduction of safety fuse, the fougasse became much more reliable and was a minor feature of defence works in military campaigns across the world. Throughout the nineteenth century and into the twentieth, the Royal Engineers' field defence instructions contained detailed descriptions of how to build a fougasse:

> the fougasse is a landmine loaded with stones, bricks etc., and arranged so that when it is fired the force of the charge is expended in driving the stones in a given direction. If charged with 80lb of powder it should throw 5 tons of bricks and stones over a surface about 160 yards long, 60 yards on either side of the axis. In easy soil two untrained men can dig out a fougasse (about 350 cubic feet) in 8 hours.

With safety fuse, defenders could be more certain that their charge would actually fire, but it was very difficult to predict precisely when it would be needed. To reach the charge at the bottom of a fougasse pit the safety fuse needed to be at least 4ft long. Add a further 6ft for the fuse to reach a concealed position from which a defender could light it and then escape. So it would take a full five minutes from lighting for the flame to burn its way through 10ft of fuse to fire the charge. In this five minutes an anticipated attack could be delayed, or a surprise one mounted.

What defenders needed was *command initiation* – the ability to fire the fougasse on command at the precise moment of their choosing – and the development of electricity provided a solution to the problem. An electrical charge, sent down an insulated wire, could produce sufficient spark to fire a gunpowder charge. The Russians claimed to have used electrically initiated mines at the siege of Silestria during the Russo–Turkish War of 1828–1829. This would suggest that they were some way ahead of the more widely recognized European and American pioneers of electricity.

The ability of the fougasse to be fired on command using an electrical charge ensured its use well into the twentieth century. The British Home Guard, short of weapons to resist an anticipated invasion by Hitler's armies in 1940, dug fougasses into key locations throughout the South of England, often with an incendiary rather than a fragmentation charge. In the 1960s, the hand-dug fougasse was superseded by a small, powerful, directional, fragmentation mine known as the Claymore (described in Chapter 7) which, although technically far superior to the fougasse, was used in exactly the same tactical context.

Fragmentation mines are deployed individually and fired on command to stop a massed attack (although they can also be fired by a victim-operated tripwire). Pressure mines are buried devices that explode when trodden on. They are laid in large numbers to inflict a small but steady stream of casualties and to induce caution in advancing soldiers. So it is useful to think of fragmentation mines as impact weapons, and pressure-operated mines as attritional weapons.

We have noted that the Chinese can make claim to having produced the first pressure-operated mine. But its fuse mechanism was so delicate and cumbersome that its utility was extremely limited. Some 300 years later, and barely more robust, was the *fladdermine* (literally flying mine), which was described by Johan Friedrich von Flemming in his military treatise *Der Vollkommene Deutsche Soldat* ('The Perfect German Soldier') of 1726. This was a victim-operated fragmentation device consisting of a ceramic container with glass and metal fragments embedded in the clay with a 2lb charge of gunpowder. It was designed to protect the glacis (an artificial slope in front of a fort) and was initiated by a flintlock mechanism attached to a low-slung tripwire. No accounts of their effectiveness in battle exist, but as an untended flintlock would remain operational for only a short period, it is safe to assume that their contribution to the overall defensive effort was nugatory.

The flintlock had been used in muskets since 1630 to fire the gunpowder charge which propelled the ball from the barrel. By the nineteenth century sports shooting had become popular, including in Scotland where the Reverend Alexander Forsyth, a keen shot, was frustrated that birds would be startled by the flintlock's flash and, in the brief pause in which it took for the gunpowder to ignite, fly off before being hit. To overcome this problem Forsyth experimented with the shock and friction-sensitive compound, mercury fulminate, that had been discovered in 1807 by Edward Howard of Norfolk. Forsyth found mercury fulminate too sensitive on its own – indeed so had Howard who was severely injured in the course of his experiments – so he mixed it with potassium chlorate, powdered glass and antimony sulphate, incorporating it in a percussion mechanism

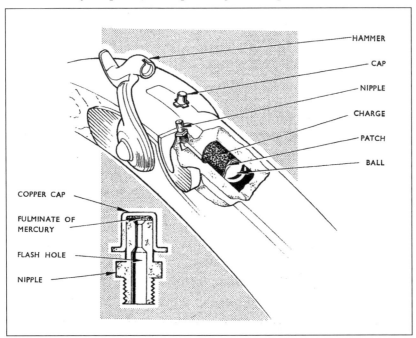

The invention of the percussion cap paved the way for the development of the pressure-operated mines used in the Crimean War and the American Civil War.

which rapidly became popular in up-market sports guns as the ball left the gun instantly, without warning birds of its arrival. His invention was also an early example of what became known as an explosive train where small amounts of sensitive explosive are used to initiate a large, less sensitive, explosive – rather as kindling is used to set larger timbers on fire.

A number of people refined Forsyth's system into a percussion cap – a small drum of copper or brass containing a tiny amount of shock-sensitive compound. Pulling a gun's trigger released a hammer which struck the percussion cap, igniting the compound and sending a small flame to ignite the gunpowder charge. By the mid-nineteenth century, many armies replaced the flintlock with the much more reliable percussion cap rifle which could be used more rapidly and worked in any weather.

The Crimean War of 1853–1856 marked a significant step in the development of pressure-operated mines on land and sea. The idea of sinking ships using gunpowder charges was not new. There had been attempts to develop naval mines for several hundred years, including by the Chinese, English and Americans. In the 1840s the Russians experimented with electrically fired naval mines. A Swedish émigré, Immanuel Nobel, went a step further and demonstrated a naval mine that did not need to be fired by an observer, but would fire on contact with a ship. Nobel was provided with a grant from the Russian Government and eventually established a factory that produced around 1,000 operational naval mines for the defence of Russian harbours during the Crimean War. These mines had charges of between 8 and 25lb of black powder, and a fuse consisting of a lead horn containing a glass tube filled with sulphuric acid over a potassium and sugar compound. On contact with a ship, the lead horn bent, breaking the glass tube, releasing the acid into the potassium and sugar resulting in a violent exothermic reaction that fired the main charge. A similar fuse was incorporated into buried mines as described by Colonel Hugh Hibbert of the Royal Fusiliers:

> These wretched Russians have discovered a new system of annoyance
> … which consists of a series of small mines or barrels of gunpowder
> let into the ground between our works and theirs, and a little tin tube

running along the ground a few inches above it, two or three inches long. This tube is filled with some composition which explodes immediately upon being touched, so that any unfortunate meandering along the grass without knowing why, suddenly finds himself going up in the air like a squib with his arms and legs going in different directions. We have had so many men blown up by these things and the grass being so long one cannot see the tube at all.

A US Military Commission to the Theater of War in Europe studied first-hand the military lessons of the Crimean War and was impressed by the mines which they described as:

A box of powder eight inches cube, contained within another box [to] secure it from wet and moisture when buried underground ... upon it rested a piece of board six inches wide, twelve inches long and one inch thick resting on four legs of thin sheet iron ... so as not to be perceived. On any slight pressure ... the thin iron supports yielded ... a glass tube containing sulphuric acid ... coming into contact with chloride of potassa [sic], causing instant combustion, and, as a consequence, explosion of the powder.

The victim-operated pressure mine was certainly used in the Crimea, but who was its creator? Immanuel Nobel had a German competitor, Moritz Herman von Jacobi. Both sought lucrative military contracts from the Russian Government using similar techniques for both naval and land mines. US researcher Norman Youngblood believes that it was Nobel who should be credited with the development of the Crimea's pressure landmines. The Nobel Prize Organisation claims: 'The naval mines designed by Immanuel Nobel were simple devices consisting of submerged wooden casks filled with gunpowder. Anchored below the surface of the Gulf of Finland, they effectively deterred the British Royal Navy from moving into firing range of St. Petersburg during the Crimean war.'[6] One hundred and forty years later the Nobel family was more publically linked with landmines when the Nobel Peace Prize was awarded to the International Campaign to Ban Landmines.

The American Civil War of 1861–1865 was on the cusp of the old and modern wars, where the tactics of Waterloo were used by armies who had at their disposal the mass-production techniques and railway transportation of the industrial age. Technical advances, tactical circumstances and a loosening of traditional codes of chivalry allowed mines, on both land and sea, to proliferate. Naval mines sank ships for the first time, electrically initiated mines were commonly used and victim-operated pressure mines were laid in the first formal minefields. The reactions to mines (often referred to as to torpedoes[7] during the American Civil War) were recorded in detail for the first time.

The key personality in the development of naval mines in general, and electrical initiation in particular, was Matthew Fontaine Maury. Maury, a Virginian, was an officer in the US Navy who resigned his commission after thirty-five years of service at the outbreak of the war to fight for the Confederates. Called upon to recommend ways of defending the South's 3,000 miles of coast with only a few ships, he proposed the use of naval mines. This was not a new idea. The US Military Commission to the Theater of War in Europe just a few years before had recommended the use of both land and naval mines. This was based on sound military logic: a cheap mine could destroy a very expensive warship, cause casualties, induce caution, disrupt offensive action, provide an element of surprise and improve the defenders' chance of success. During the war the statistics backed up the logic: Confederate naval mines sank or damaged forty-three Union ships.

Maury first demonstrated the potential of naval mines to the Secretary of the Confederate Navy on the James River in June 1861. He initiated it 'using a spark passed through an electrical cable [and] up went a column of water fifteen or twenty feet [resulting in] many dead or stunned fish'. The device had its first operational success on the Yazoo River, a tributary of the Mississippi, on 12 December 1862. The victim was one of the new ironclads, USS *Cairo*, which sank within minutes after two electrical mines were fired by a Confederate party led by Lieutenant Issac N. Brown who reported that he was torn by conflicting emotions, 'much as a school boy whose practical joke has taken a more serious turn than expected'. The USS *Cairo* was the first ship ever to be sunk by a mine. In 1964 she was raised, preserved, and put on display in Vicksberg National Park.

Brown not only sank the first ship by electrical–initiated mine, he also planted, together with Maury, the war's first electrically initiated mine to defend a position at Randolf's Bluff above Columbus on the Mississippi. The mines had squat iron casings with handles that resembled cooking pots, were filled with 4lb grape-shot artillery shells and were planted in clusters.

The Confederate position at Columbus was abandoned before the mines could be fired and the advancing Union army was warned of their presence by deserters, scores of mines being discovered after patches of disturbed soil were investigated. One of the most popular papers of the time, *Harper's Weekly*, in its 29 March 1862 edition, described: 'infernal machines [with which] whole regiments could be blown up without even a chance of escape'. It was the first time that the media had condemned the use of mines.

During the American Civil War, whilst Maury made his name with naval mines and electrical initiation, Brigadier Gabriel J. Rains made his with landmines and pressure fuzes. Rains graduated from West Point in 1827 and served in the infantry during the war against the Seminole Indians in Florida, where he experimented with booby traps but achieved little success. He joined the Confederate Army at the outbreak of war, motivated by bitter feelings towards the Union, especially after the shelling of his home in North Carolina. A colleague wrote of him: 'He would not use such a weapon in ordinary warfare, but has no scruples in resorting to any means of defence against an army of abolitionists invading our country for the purpose, avowed, of extermination.' The Rains pressure fuse used a very similar mixture to that pioneered by Forsyth for percussion caps; a pressure of only 7lb on a thin copper cap was sufficient to explode the sensitive mixture. The fuzes were inserted into artillery shells, often the spherical type with a polygonal cavity which provided internal weak points that would burst when the gunpowder charge exploded. The durability of the design was demonstrated in 1960 when five of these devices were recovered near Mobile, Alabama, reportedly with the powder 'still quite dangerous', although it is highly unlikely that these mines could have functioned.

On a fine spring morning on 4 May 1862, at Yorktown, Virginia, a Union cavalry detachment was scouting along the road to Richmond.

Without warning an explosion beneath a horse killed the animal and injured its rider. A mine had claimed its first victim in the American Civil War. Union forces at Yorktown had besieged a much smaller Confederate force for the previous month and had planned for a decisive artillery barrage on 5 May, but the Confederates had slipped away during the previous night. Word soon spread that they had left mines and booby traps, which as Rains explained 'have a moral effect in checking the advance of the enemy [and] to save our sick'. Appreciating the threat that the mines posed to their own side, each one was marked by a small red warning flag a few paces away. Charles A. Phillips of the 5th Massachusetts Artillery wrote: 'a blood stain on the ground where a man was blown up ... and a little red flag ten feet from it, admonished us to be careful. The rebels have shown great ingenuity for our especial benefit.' The mines caused perhaps three dozen casualties and delayed by three days the Union advance on to Williamsburg.

The Union General McClellen was outraged, telling his superiors, 'The rebels have been guilty of the most murderous and barbarous conduct in placing torpedoes [mines] within the abandoned works near wells and springs, near flag staffs, magazines, telegraph offices, in carpet bags, barrels of flour etc. ... I shall make the prisoners remove them at their peril.' As we shall see, McClellen's outrage and his use of prisoners to clear mines, was to be repeated in wars for many years to come.

It was not only McClellen who was deeply disturbed by the use of mines. Rains soon found himself clicking his heels before his superior, General James Longstreet, who took a very dim view of the episode, forbidding Rains from laying more mines as he did not consider it 'a proper or effective method of war'. But Rains felt strongly about the issue and appealed to the War Department. Mines, he argued, were as effective as a rearguard but would not result in the loss of their own men, and he claimed that McClellen's men were digging a tunnel mine under the Confederate position, entitling him to prepare mines of a smaller scale. The debate was settled by the Secretary of War, George W. Randolph, who decided that mines could be used. Sensitive to military protocol and not wishing to undermine Longstreet's authority, Rains was temporarily transferred to work on the defences of the James and Appomattox Rivers.

The impact of the Yorktown mining incident, the success of naval mines and the steady advances by Union forces ensured that Rains' services were soon needed again on land. He was provided with a budget of $20,000 in 1863 which was increased to $350,000 the following year, allowing mines to be used in increasing numbers. The same year the light touch required to handle the sensitive fuzes eluded Rains and one exploded in his hand leaving him 'scarcely able to write his name'.[8]

Towards the end of the war mines were buried in larger groups and started to develop a degree of formality. Minefields of victim-operated pressure mines based on artillery shells were laid in front of Fort McAllister near Savannah where a garrison of 230 was attacked by 4,000 of Sherman's men in December 1864. The fort fell in fifteen minutes, but eight Union soldiers were killed and a further eighty were injured by mines. After the battle Sherman made Confederate prisoners remove the mines, a decision that infuriated the Confederate Commander, Major George W. Anderson, who thought 'this hazardous duty [was] an unwarrantable and improper treatment of his men'. Sherman was unmoved. It was not until the 1949 Geneva Convention that the forced use of prisoners of war for mine clearance was expressly forbidden.

In one of the final battles of the war – the defence of Richmond – Rains personally supervised the planting of 1,298 mines in fields around the city. Each mine was marked by a small red flag on a pole a yard high, which was replaced by a lantern covered by red flannel at night, a clear indication that without adequate marking mines were a serious threat to the defenders too. In other battles mines were not so effectively marked. Encountering mines at Spanish Fort Alabama a Union Officer reported, 'The carelessness evinced by the rebels in marking places of their deposit is most culpable as many could not be found and are liable at any time to injure persons', a comment that would be pertinent in many conflict zones of the late twentieth century.

The Union forces were outraged by mines when they first

Explosion of a torpedo.

Several thousand mines, known as torpedoes, were laid by Confederate forces during the American Civil War. Union General George McClellan thought their use was 'murderous and barbarous' (from Harper's Weekly, *24 May 1867).*

encountered them, but gradually developed a degree of acceptance. H.U. Dowd of 114th Ohio Regiment noted in his dairy in April 1865: 'Nothing going on of note today … the boys anxious to go north ... one man got his leg blowed off by a torpedo.' Even Sherman had a change of attitude on the road to Richmond: 'I now decide that the use of the torpedo is justifiable in war in advance of an army. But after the adversary has gained the country by fair and warlike means ... the case entirely changes. The use of torpedoes in blowing up our cars and the road after they are in our procession is simply malicious.' On this latter aspect Sherman had strong views: 'If torpedoes are found in the possession of an enemy to our rear, you may cause them to be put on the ground and tested by wagon-loads of prisoners. Of course an enemy cannot complain of his own traps.'

Another, less tangible, but highly important aspect of the use of mines was their psychological effect. As a Union Officer expressed it: 'The knowledge that these shells [mines] were scattered in every direction would necessarily produce its effect on the troops who never knew when to expect an explosion or where to go to avoid one.' The psychological impact of mines could often be more important than their physical effect.

During the Civil War, several thousand mines were laid and they caused hundreds of casualties, although this was a fraction of the Union's total of 360,000 dead and the few hours or days of delay that they imposed on the Union advance counted for little in any strategic sense. But they had some local, tactical importance. The Confederates used them to compensate for their smaller forces, as they observed: 'Such was the protection they afforded that only two companies per mile were sometimes left to hold works rear of these torpedoes ... elsewhere dummy minefields were frequently established ... the fact that such mines were never passed over by an assaulting column proved that they did their work.' It was the mine's ability to provide economies in defence whilst imposing delays and casualties on attackers that ensured that they would be used in great numbers in future wars.

Before moving to the next stage of the development of mines, let us briefly untangle some common misunderstandings surrounding their origin. The term mine is derived from the practice of tunnelling beneath a defender's position. Both laying mines and digging tunnel mines (which are sometimes also called landmines, and to further confuse matters some air-dropped bombs are known as mines) involve the use of buried explosive, but there the similarities end. The key tactical difference is that mines are weapons of defence, whereas tunnel mines are weapons of attack. The key technical differences are that mines are generally victim operated and buried en masse a few centimetres below the ground. Tunnel mines are fired on command

and dug individually many metres below the ground.

Tunnel mines were used against fortified positions since the construction of the first defensive wall around Jericho some 8,000 years before Christ. Stone ramparts offered protection for defenders and provided a platform from which to use weapons against attackers. This left attackers with three choices: they could starve out defenders, which could take a very long time against a well-provisioned garrison; attempt to scale the walls, which was very difficult against a well-organized defence; or they could collapse the walls by tunnel mining beneath them.

From a concealed area beyond the range of defenders' weapons, attackers would dig a tunnel to the castle walls where they would hollow out a large cavity. This cavity was supported by timbers which were then burnt or pulled down, collapsing the walls above it. Attackers would then pour through the breach to assault the garrison. Tunnel mines were slow to dig, but faster than waiting for the garrison to run out of food. They were hazardous to construct, but less so than a direct assault on the walls. And they could be highly effective – in 332 BC Alexander the Great took the city of Gaza after breaching its walls using mines and slaughtered all the men for putting up such stout resistance.

Defenders did not always passively await their fate, as Hamlet said:

> For 'tis the sport to have the engineer
> Hoist with his own petard: and 't shall go hard
> But I will delve one yard below their mines,
> And blow them at the moon.

In other words, they dug counter-tunnel mines to attack the attackers before the walls were breached. At the Castle of St Andrews in Scotland the remains can be seen of a mine and a successful countermine dug through solid rock during the siege of 1546–7.

The introduction of gunpowder made tunnel mining much more effective. Burning timbers to collapse walls was no easy process as there was limited oxygen to sustain fire in the poorly ventilated tunnels. Gunpowder did not need oxygen; the greater its confinement, the more powerful its effects, and less effort was required as it literally blew up, rather than relying on walls collapsing into a large, painstakingly dug cavity.

The introduction of gunpowder to tunnel mines occurred during a period when guns became more efficient. The breaching of Constantinople's great walls by cannon in 1453 demonstrated the vulnerability of high castle walls to cannon fire and caused military engineers to rethink how to defend towns and garrisons. In essence they swapped height for depth. The result was the introduction of the low, star-shaped fort with a succession of broad moats and angular bastions. The broad bastions provided much stouter resistance to direct-fire guns and also greatly reduced the threat of mining. The increased depth of defences meant that tunnels had to be much longer, large moats forced tunnels much deeper, and low bastions were much more difficult to blow up than tall walls. Vauban, the famous French military siege engineer, designed scores of these fortifications around Europe. But like a gamekeeper turned poacher, he also developed a system for besieging fortifications using a series of parallel trenches connected by saps (deep narrow trenches), encircling a fort with ever-decreasing circles.

Tunnel mines reappeared as a means of breaking the deadlock in trench warfare on the Western Front during the First World War.[9] The largest ever tunnel mine, consisting of around 450 tons of explosives, was detonated, despite some countermining successes, on Messines Ridge on 7 June 1916. Hundreds of Germans were killed in the blast and the Allies were able to secure the ridge for themselves. Tunnel mining was widespread along the Western Front with over 30,000 miners engaged in the British lines alone. At the peak of activity in June 1916 an average of three tunnel mines a day were fired by the British. Despite this frenetic activity it was conceded by the Royal Engineers after the war that 'the result achieved was seldom commensurate with the expenditure of personnel, material and time involved.'

The success of tunnel mining had always depended on surprise, but in the First World War two inventions made this very difficult to achieve. The first was the geophone listening device which, with the aid of compass bearings, made counter-tunnel mining much more accurate. The second was the introduction of reconnaissance aircraft from which spoil from mines could easily be spotted. But ultimately the use of tunnel mines stopped because static defences, the tactical environment in which they were used, were abandoned in favour of mobile defences. Defenders seldom occupied a position for long enough for attackers to make the laborious process of tunnelling and mining worthwhile.

Notes

1 The introduction of gunpowder brought about profound changes in the way battles were fought. Guns were first used in battle on the European battlefield in the thirteenth century and by the seventeenth century the demand for gunpowder was so great that in response to declining supplies of potassium nitrate Charles I felt the need to institute extraordinary measures to remedy the situation. He ordered his subjects to 'carefully and constantly preserve all the urine of man during the year and all the stale of beasts ... and that they be careful to use the best means of gathering together and preserving the urine and the stale'.

2 There are claims that as well as the Chinese, the Indians, Arabs and Persians knew of gunpowder before the Europeans. Bacon was a scientist and linguist and there is debate whether he discovered gunpowder by experiment or by translation of Chinese or Arabic scripts. Either way, he described his discovery as a substance by which 'the sound of thunder may be artificially produced in the air with greater resulting horror than if it had been produced by natural causes.' He coded the details of its composition to ensure that its secrets were revealed only to a select, educated few, although within a few decades, knowledge of gunpowder was widespread.

3 Its name comes from a French type of flat bread. Once emplaced all that was visible of the fougasse was a low disc of stones, which resembled – with a degree of imagination – unleavened bread.

4 Le Blond, M., *The Military Engineer or a treatise on the attack and defence of fortified places*, London, 1759.

5 Safety fuse remains in both civilian and military explosive inventories with a design largely unchanged since Bickford's day.

6 http://nobelprize.org/alfred-nobel

7 The term torpedo comes from the Latin and refers to the torpor caused by the sting of an electric eel.

8 Perry, M.F., *Infernal Machines*, Louisiana State University Press, 1985, p. 41. Milton Perry's book, first published in 1965, is the seminal work on mine (and submarine) warfare during the American Civil War.

9 They were also used in the American Civil War where Union forces dug under the Confederate earthworks at Petersburg in 1864.

Chapter 3

High-Explosive Mines

—~~~—

Equally dangerous to friend or foe and extremely
dangerous to pick up when no longer required.
Major Bucknill, Royal Engineers, 1884

By the mid-nineteenth century the strength of gunpowder had been increased by changing the proportions of its ingredients and a degree of resistance to atmospheric moisture was provided by polishing the powder's grains. But its power, that appeared so phenomenal in the thirteenth century, was considered frustratingly inadequate by the nineteenth century. The main demand for more explosive power and greater reliability came not from the military, but from the world of civil engineering. The Industrial Revolution required better communications, and the need to cut train tunnels through the Alps and the Rockies stimulated scientific research into explosives.

One of the earliest replacements for gunpowder was found in 1846 by the German chemist Christian Schonbein. He mixed nitric and sulphuric acids into cellulose, which occurs naturally in fibrous material such as cotton, making nitrocellulose, or as he called it – guncotton. Guncotton could be initiated by a flame and it was two to four times as powerful as gunpowder, whilst producing much less smoke and residue. Guncotton factories were quickly licensed across Europe. But tragedy struck in the 1847. An accident in a guncotton works in Faversham, England, demolished the factory and, as the owner wrote: 'Eighteen persons were killed by that explosion, ten only could be recognised, the remainder were literally blown to atoms and scattered with the materials in all directions.' There were further explosions in guncotton factories in Europe and its production was halted until 1865 when a safe means of producing guncotton was patented by Sir Frederick Augustus Abel, professor of chemistry at the Royal Military Academy at Woolwich. Abel's guncotton proved safe and could be pressed into any shape for use in munitions. It was adopted as the standard British military explosive in the 1870s and formed the main charge in most British mines until after the First World War.

At around the same time that Schonbein was discovering guncotton, a much more powerful explosive, known as nitroglycerine, was discovered in 1847 by an Italian, Ascanio Sobrero, a doctor turned chemist at the University of Turin. Pure nitroglycerin is a colourless, oily, somewhat toxic liquid with a sharp sweet taste, made by adding glycerine, a product of soap, to a mixture of concentrated nitric and sulphuric acids. Sobrero was a man of medicine rather than war. He developed nitroglycerin for vasodilation – the widening of the blood vessels – to treat angina pectoris, and it remains in medical use to this day. But nitroglycerine's other property became apparent when a sample he was working on blew up injuring his face and hands. Unsurprisingly, he developed little interest in pursuing its explosive properties and concentrated on medical applications.

On initiation, nitroglycerine produces a large volume of hot gasses accompanied by a sharp increase in pressure. Gunpowder does this too, but the scale is altogether different. Gunpowder *explodes* producing pressures of up to 6,000 atmospheres in a few milliseconds. To emphasise the difference, nitroglycerine (like all high explosives) is said to *detonate* (from the Latin *tonare*: to thunder) and produces pressures of over 250,000 atmospheres in a few *micro*seconds. Therefore gunpowder is classed as a low explosive and nitroglycerine as a high explosive. Most people are familiar with the bang made by the gunpowder in fireworks. This may seem loud, but the sound of high explosive is very much louder still, highly distinctive and intensely shocking. Depending on how far you are from a detonation, you see a white flash, and instantly feel a thump on your chest as the blast wave passes you (which can cause serious lung injuries), followed by an ear-splitting crack (rather than a bang) the volume of which is almost beyond human comprehension.

The power of nitroglycerine was obvious, but it was difficult to harness as its response to initiation by an open flame was inconsistent. It was therefore very dangerous. Here the story returns to the Nobel family and in particular Alfred, who helped his father to make mines for the Russians during the Crimean War. Alfred Nobel was the product of a first-class education, paid for by his family's successful businesses. He was sent abroad to study chemistry and whilst in Paris he met the Italian, Sobrero. Unlike the disfigured Italian, Nobel saw the explosive rather than the medical potential of nitroglycerine. Back in Sweden in the 1860s, Nobel started to manufacture nitroglycerine on a small scale. In 1864, he found that a small amount of gunpowder mixed with mercury fulminate (which Forsyth had used in the first percussion caps) could reliably detonate nitroglycerine. Having established the principle, he set about producing safe, easy-to-use *detonators*. Tiny amounts of his mixture were packed in a small copper tube about 6mm in diameter, closed at one end with the other left open for safety fuse (of William Bickford's design) to be inserted. A flame from the lit safety fuse would detonate the fulminate mixture which in turn would detonate the nitroglycerine. This is another example of an explosive train. Detonators are used in all landmines to set off the high-explosive charge.

But there was another problem. As a liquid, nitroglycerine remained difficult to handle, and whilst the detonator permitted nitroglycerine to be initiated on command, it retained a habit of detonating unpredictably. The story of the development of explosives is peppered with violent accidents and it hit close to home in 1864 when Alfred Nobel's brother was killed along with four others, when nitroglycerine accidentally detonated at the family works in Heleneburg, Sweden.

In 1867, Nobel stumbled upon a way of taming nitroglycerine. Kieselgur or diamataceous earth, a soft chalk-like rock made of fossilized diatoms – a type of shelled algae – was used as packing around flasks of nitroglycerine in transit. When inspecting a damaged

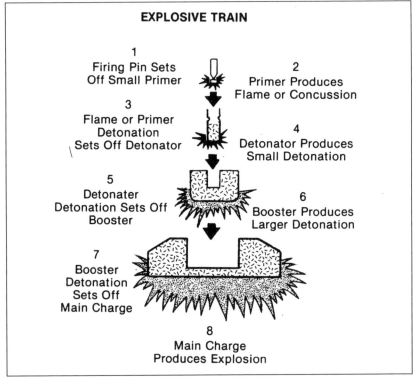

EXPLOSIVE TRAIN

1
Firing Pin Sets
Off Small Primer

2
Primer Produces
Flame or Concussion

3
Flame or Primer
Detonation
Sets Off Detonator

4
Detonator Produces
Small Detonation

5
Detonater
Detonation Sets Off
Booster

6
Booster Produces
Larger Detonation

7
Booster
Detonation
Sets Off
Main Charge

8
Main Charge
Produces Explosion

The explosive train is a sequence of explosives of different properties found within all mines.

flask, Nobel noticed that kieselguhr absorbed the liquid nitroglycerine and discovered that the resulting malleable solid mixture could be detonated reliably. It was slightly less powerful than liquid nitroglycerine but it was stable. This new high explosive was to become one of the most famous brand names of all times: Dynamite (from the Greek *dynamis* meaning power). Dynamite was ideal for mining and quarrying, although it needed to be stored carefully or sensitive crystals could form on it creating a dangerous situation. Providing optimum storage conditions in the field was difficult so the military preferred to use guncotton, but the additional power of dynamite was appealing if it could be harnessed in a more durable form.

The solution was found in the German chemical industry where trinitrotoluene, a lightweight, solid material was developed in 1863 as a yellow dye. TNT, as it became better known, was not initially understood to have explosive properties because it was very difficult to detonate – a booster charge or a stronger detonator was required.

But this insensitivity was an ideal quality for shells which had to withstand the shock of being fired from an artillery piece. From 1902 it was adopted by the German military as the standard shell filling and in 1916 by the British. TNT also had the ideal qualities for use in mines. Its insensitivity to shock meant that shells landing nearby did not easily cause sympathetic detonation. It was powerful, stable in a wide range of conditions, unaffected by damp when stored, lightweight, easily melted for filling any shape container, and was cheap to make. From the end of the First World War TNT was the standard explosive used in most mines.

High explosives offered, weight for weight, a much bigger bang than gunpowder. Whereas a kilo or two of gunpowder might amputate a man's leg, the same result could be achieved with a couple of hundred grams of high explosive. But although mines could be smaller, quicker to lay, more difficult to locate and much lighter on the logistics chain, the arrival of high explosives did not spawn the development of a new generation of landmines overnight. Mines demonstrated their greatest potential at sea and most new investment went into naval rather than land mines during the second half of the nineteenth century. By the First World War mines had become an established and sophisticated part of naval warfare. During the war the Allies laid over 150,000 mines in the North Sea accounting for 150 enemy warships. By contrast, no army entered the First World War with mass-produced landmines in their arsenals, and whilst some were used during the war, they were very much a marginal weapon. Naval minefields were used strategically and were capable of sinking very expensive warships, significantly reducing an enemy's war-fighting capacity. Landmines were a tactical weapon taking out only a small proportion of an attacking force.

Although a marginal weapon, mines were used in many of the conflicts during the second half of the nineteenth century. During the colonial wars the British Army used mines to defend positions against native warriors. Often these were improvised in the field and lacked the technical sophistication of those used in the American Civil War. This was probably because the well-armed, highly disciplined, red-coated Christian soldiers did not expect to have to mount a serious defence against native warriors. These mines consisted of a rifle trigger mechanism which fired a detonator, or a blank round, to initiate a guncotton charge. They were buried leaving the trigger, sometimes attached to a tripwire, above the ground to catch unsuspecting victims. The trigger mechanism, rather than pressure, made them inefficient, and the exposed mechanism often became blocked with sand making them unreliable. One of the earliest recorded uses of mines during the colonial wars was during the Zulu War of 1879 when they were used to protect road-building parties. These may have provided some small comfort to isolated units who, following the Battle of Isandlwana, would have been acutely aware of the effectiveness of Zulu warriors.

In contrast to the sober deliberation about the use of mines in the American Civil War, the British were positively gleeful about them. Five months into the siege of Khartoum in July 1884, an excited General Gordon wrote: 'Landmines are the things for defence in the future. We have covered our [defensive] works with them and they have deterred all attacks and they have done much execution.'

Behind Gordon's bravado there was a serious point. He was trapped in Khartoum with a force of 7,000, surrounded by a Sudanese Mahdist army of perhaps 50,000. Khartoum was protected to the north and east by the Blue Nile and to the west by the White Nile. The south however was open country with few natural defences and it was this approach that he fortified with whatever he could lay his hands on, including wire entanglements, caltrops and mines. The siege lasted for ten months at which point, the Mahdists were spurred into action by the approach of a relieving force, and took advantage of the lower level of the Nile to ford the river and attack the city. The field fortifications and mines may have deterred an attack from the south, but the entire garrison was slaughtered anyway.

Whilst they may have 'done much execution' to the enemy, mines also took out a few of their own. Lieutenant Asquith, Royal Engineers, laid mines to prevent snipers occupying positions overlooking Khartoum's fortifications. On checking his devices he was 'hoist by his own petard' as 'poor Asquith had evidently been on his hands and knees scraping to find the mine, for only his legs from knee to foot were found together untouched.' The sharp-eyed Sudanese had apparently spotted the mines and moved them to catch the Engineers.

Mines provided another source of danger. Major Bucknill, writing in the *Royal Engineers Journal* in 1884 claimed 'simple mechanical [victim-operated] mines are equally dangerous to friend or foe and extremely dangerous to pick up when no longer required. To clear a space of purely mechanical mines it is necessary to drive sheep over the ground.[1] This is a theme that reoccurs throughout the history of mines and the problems of alerting friendly forces to the presence of their own mines and of clearing redundant mines have never been entirely overcome.

To mitigate against the dangers of pressure mines the *Royal Engineers Journal* recommended in 1886 that electrically fired mines 'should in almost every case be preferred to mechanical methods'. Not everyone entirely agreed. Commander Kingscote, in a letter published in the *Journal*, claimed: 'For ordinary purposes mines must be electrical, but in warfare against savage nations, mechanical mines are very useful in fighting natives.' It is unclear whether Kingscote's view stemmed from tactical circumstances, or a lower code of military ethics employed in 'savage nations'. But in general, the British appeared to have few moral inhibitions when using mines, unlike the Americans who, mindful of their Civil War experience, maintained that 'it is not permissible to plant such mines on any ground which is not obviously prepared for defence' in their *US Engineer Field Manual*.

The British used mines in the Boer War of 1899–1903. At the siege of Mafeking in 1899 a small British garrison led by Colonel Baden-Powell, who went on to found the Scouting movement, prepared defences around the town, including fake barbed wire. Short stakes were driven into the ground and the defenders simulated stringing wire between them and stepping over it. The Boers, several hundred metres away, could not tell that the wire did not exist. More pertinently the defences included extensive trenches and a convincing series of fake minefields alongside electrically initiated mines which contained 4lb of guncotton. The mines were not fired and, against all expectations, the town resisted the siege. This is not overwhelming evidence of the deterrent effect of minefields, but they certainly contributed to the overall defence, as they had done at Khartoum. Firmer evidence of their effectiveness was found along the Blomfontein–Kruger railway. Mines were laid beside the track by Lieutenant Musgrove, Royal Engineers, who noted: 'Although the line had been injured for eight successive nights before the mine was laid, it was never interfered with ... after the first explosion.' Furthermore: 'Mines were laid [along the roads] at nearly every culvert and had good moral effect, as after this was done, the Boers never attempted to destroy them.' In the twentieth century it would be the guerrilla forces that used mines very effectively to attack much larger occupying forces.

In the Russo-Japanese War of 1904–1905 both the Russians and the Japanese lost several of their major battleships to each other's naval mines which significantly altered the course of the war at sea. On land it was a different story. The Russians were besieged in Port Arthur, which eventually fell, and spent much of the war on the defensive, often in successive lines of trenches covered by machine-gun and artillery fire, a foretaste of the First World War style of combat. They had used mines during the Crimean War and did so again in Manchuria. These included electrically fired fougasses and pressure-operated mines. Japanese Lieutenant Tadayoshi Sakurai referred to the density of the field fortifications: 'Each spot was made still more uncomfortable by ground-mines, pitfalls, wire entanglements etc. There was hardly a space where even an ant could get through unmolested.' Captain Bannerman, a British military observer at Port Arthur, was less impressed: 'The destruction caused by Russian landmines ... has been insignificant, if not absolutely nil.' His American counterpart, Captain Toefer, added that: 'On the whole, the moral effect which the detonation that a mine produces has, like always hitherto, been greater than the material loss.' So mines had a spectacular effect at sea, but had little impact on land.

During the First World War armies were paralysed in rows of opposing trenches, raked by machine-gun fire and drenched by artillery shells. Away from the cover of their trenches, whole battalions were cut down in a matter of minutes in a blizzard of shrapnel and bullets. The stalemate of the trenches had precipitated the revival of tunnelling and mining, but the style of warfare created few circumstances in which the anti-personnel mine had utility. Early in the war the British had experimented with tripwire-operated mines, within barbed-wire entanglements in no man's land, but they were quickly phased out as they proved equally dangerous to their own troops. The Germans protected their lines with caltrops and wolf holes: sharpened sticks placed in knee-deep pits, techniques that Caesar would have immediately recognized. But mines were dangerous to lay in no man's land, easily disrupted by artillery fire, added no defensive advantage over that of the machine gun and could inhibit counter-attack.

Mines, or more correctly, booby traps, were used when defensive positions were abandoned to delay enemy occupation. The distinction between landmines and booby traps is often quite fine. Mines are mass produced and are normally deployed in groups. Booby traps are improvised and are normally deployed individually. Both are victim operated: mines by activating a tripwire or by the pressure of a footfall; booby traps by employing cunning or deception to harm their victim, such as a charge set to detonate when a door is opened, or when a rifle is picked up. The term booby originates from the bird of the same name. A member of the gannet family, boobies have a slightly comical facial expression and their gullible behaviour allows them to be caught by hand.

The British evacuation from Gallipoli in 1915 provided an insight into booby trap preparations:

The men in the trenches spent the last day turning every dugout into a death trap and the most innocent looking things into infernal machines. Some dugouts would blow up when the doors were opened. A drafting table had several memorandum books lying on it each with electrical connections to an explosive charge sufficient to blow up an entire platoon. A gramophone wound up and with the record on, ready to be started was left in one dugout, so the end of the tune meant death to the listeners. Piles of bully beef, turned into diabolical engines of destruction, lay scattered about. In front of the trenches lay miles of trip wires. Hundreds of rifles lay on top of the parapet, with strings tied to the triggers, supporting a tin can into which water from another tin dripped. Flares were arranged the same way. Really, I never thought the British Tommy possessed such diabolical ingenuity.

To prevent the rapid occupation of their trenches, the Germans developed pressure fuzes that could be screwed into artillery shells. These were buried vertically in the bottom of trenches, with the fuze level with the ground, and were supplemented by delayed time-action charges – strictly speaking neither a mine nor a booby trap. These charges were artillery shells fitted with a chemical fuze that detonated the shell up to forty-eight hours after it was set. British officers advancing in November 1918 into trenches containing booby traps, mines and long-delay charges noted, rather like Union forces advancing towards Richmond, that 'progress was much slower ... and the opportunity to turn an unprepared retreat into a rout could not be taken advantage of'. So the Germans used mines to buy time. The practice of mining abandoned trenches in the late stages of the war was so widespread that Article 8 of the Armistice stated: 'The German command shall be responsible for revealing within the period of forty-eight hours after the signing of the armistice all mines or delayed action fuses on territory evacuated by the German troops and shall assist in their discovery and destruction.'

In German East (now Tanzania) and South-West (now Namibia) Africa the much more mobile form of warfare precipitated the use of mines by the Germans to defend their positions, and as a means of closing roads. Von Lettow Vorbeck, the brilliant commander of German forces in German East Africa (now Tanzania), improvised mines from grenades and shells initiated by rifle trigger mechanisms (similar to those used by the British in Sudan). Few of these functioned as soldiers, terrified of premature explosions, would leave the safety catch on.

In German South-West Africa some areas were heavily and elaborately mined. Louis Botha, the South African Prime Minister (who had fought against the British in the Boer War) wrote to the German Commander, Vicktor Franke, complaining that the use of mines and the poisoning of wells were 'outrages against the rules of civilized conflict'. Franke replied that mines were legal and that he had a right to poison wells as long as they marked them as such. The Germans used a pipe mine that was

> made by packing dynamite into a T piece of ordinary quarter inch [sic] water pipe. A glass tube in the cross piece held the detonating compound. A thin steel rod in the long part of the T had one end resting on the glass tube: the other projected about half an inch above the ground when the mine was buried. When stepped on the rod broke and detonated the charge.[1]

The small explosive charge in these mines would wound rather than kill anyone who trod on them and they may have been the first operational device deliberately calculated to have this effect. It was not only Botha who was outraged by the use of mines, South African troops declared them 'a very unfair and unsportsman-like way of fighting' and some had to be prevented from killing prisoners who had defended their positions with them.

The earliest anti-tank mines were improvised from artillery shells.

Whilst opportunities to use mines against personnel during the First World War were limited, the introduction of the tank presented new possibilities. Throughout the war attempts to endow the offensive with superior strength were largely unsuccessful. The machine gun, so effective in defence, was difficult to use in attack. Intense artillery bombardment did little to weaken defences and made the ground difficult for attackers. Poison gas proved too capricious a weapon and the new air reconnaissance capability robbed both sides of surprise attacks as troop concentrations could easily be spotted. The stalemate was broken by tanks that could provide attacking momentum by combining armoured protection with firepower. The first tanks were introduced to the Western Front by the British in September 1916. For the remainder of the war, tanks were used in ever-increasing numbers, gradually becoming an important factor in Allied victories.

To defend against tanks the Germans first tried to flood land to create an impassable swamp. This could only be achieved in a few areas so they then created artificial obstacles such as wide ditches or stout wooden stockades to block a tank's passage. But impeding movement was insufficient – a means of destroying tanks was needed. The Germans experimented with tank pits – large holes with a camouflaged wooden lid designed to break under the weight of a tank causing it to drop into the pit – but these proved quite impratical. The indirect fire of artillery had very little chance of hitting a tank, and machine-gun bullets simply rattled off the side of the machines, although doubtless unnerving the crews. So the Germans developed the first anti-tank gun, the 13.2mm *Tank Abwehr Gewehr*, capable of piercing 20mm of armour at 100m, which had some success in the later stages of the war.

To supplement direct-fire weapons, the Germans also began to develop anti-tank mines. Early designs were based on artillery shells dug into the ground and covered with boards to form a wide pressure plate. Another design featured a pivoting board that, upon pressure from a tank track, pulled a pin from a spring-loaded striker and initiated a shell. These early anti-tank mines were constructed by front-line soldiers and proved unreliable and time consuming to lay.

Soon after the Battle of Cambrai in November 1917, to increase efficiency, the Germans started to mass produce anti-tank mines. They consisted of a tarred wooden box measuring 13in by 9in square and 6in high, filled with about 8lb of guncotton. A spring-retained bar across the top of the mine was depressed by the weight of the tank to cause it to function. The guncotton charge was sufficiently large to break the tracks of a tank, immobilizing rather than destroying it. Laying anti-tank mines was an infantry function with each German battalion forming its own mine-laying unit consisting of one NCO and five other ranks. Initially mines were laid in small groups on roads or approaches to strongpoints. Later in the war the Germans, demonstrating characteristic thoroughness, developed a standard minefield to stop massed tank attacks. It consisted of two rows of anti-tank mines offset at 2m spacings behind a barbed-wire picket fence. Attached to every third picket by a wire was an explosive charge, buried 2m from the fence on the enemy side of the wire.

Anticipating the appearance of German tanks, the Royal Engineers produced a mine in 1918. This was a wooden box, 18in by 14in square and 8in high, containing 14lb of guncotton. It was initiated by depressing a hinged lid that operated a firing lever connected to a detonator. The British laid extensive minefields along a considerable part of the Third and Fifth Army fronts. However, the Germans fielded less than twenty tanks during the entire war and none of them encountered Allied mines.

Neither the British nor the Germans used anti-personnel mines to protect anti-tank mines. Tanks were armoured against machine-gun fire and deployed to breach defences for troops on foot. It was far too dangerous for troops to clear paths ahead of tanks. The common misconception that anti-personnel mines were used to protect anti-tank mines on the Western Front probably stems from the low pressure required to operate anti-tank mines of the period, often as little as 50kg. So anti-tank mines could be initiated by troops on foot as the Germans discovered in March 1918, when a British officer noted that they 'began a methodical attack ... but ... their leading lines entered an anti-tank minefield and exploded some buried charges. A panic ensued and the advance was brought to a halt for a considerable time.'

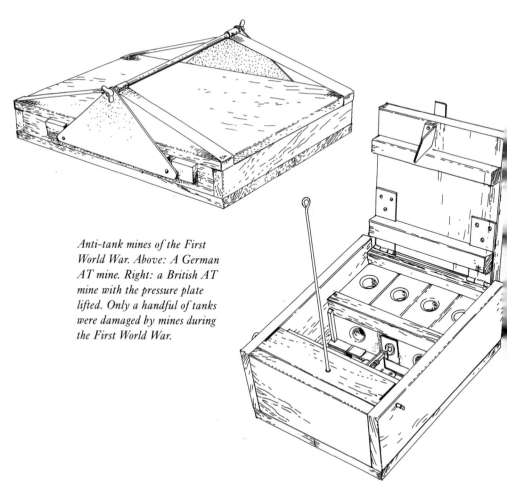

Anti-tank mines of the First World War. Above: A German AT mine. Right: a British AT mine with the pressure plate lifted. Only a handful of tanks were damaged by mines during the First World War.

Only a handful of tanks encountered mines during the war, the most significant example of their effectiveness occurring in September 1918 when the American 301st Tank Battalion using British Mark V tanks ran into a minefield. Of the thirty-five tanks used in the attack by the Battalion, ten were damaged by mines. The incident was doubly unfortunate as the minefield had been laid by the British some months earlier. An official report noted that the effect of these mines, which consisted of trench mortar shells, was 'greater than any German tank mines which have been encountered. Not only were the tracks and rollers shattered, but also the floor and main girders were displaced.'

Some context is needed to explain the modest impact of these early anti-tank mines. Tanks were introduced late in the war. In 1916, a total of sixty tanks were in action on five days, in 1917, 988 tanks were in action on twenty-two days, and in 1918, 2,245 tanks were in action on fifty-five days. So, until the last months of the war, these lumbering mechanical beasts were a rarity on the battlefield. And it is important to recognize that the tank did not open the road to Berlin. They enjoyed limited success, and then only late in the war; but their potential was clear. The same was true of the anti-tank mine; despite damaging few tanks, they were clearly a useful addition to an arsenal. That the Allies laid minefields in anticipation of the Germans fielding tanks in numbers was recognition that minefields were one of the most effective ways of stopping tanks. And their concern about the mine threat to the tank was sufficient for mine rollers to be developed. These were attached to a tank using a bowsprit, and were designed to detonate mines under their own weight ahead of the tank's tracks. Rollers arrived too late to see action but they were tested in France early in 1919.

Paradoxically, it was the Allies who neglected the mine after the war whilst the Germans gradually became its master. After 'the war to end all wars', the Allies had little appetite, or money, for investing in military technology, so it was unsurprising that there was little advance in the development of the mine. The war had raised many questions about the nature of future conflict given the new dimensions of aerial and armoured combat, but only a few were prepared to look for answers. The most prominent British military theorist of the post-war period was Basil Liddell Hart, who had served on the Western Front during the war. Liddell Hart wrote a doctrine for mobile warfare based on the mobility and firepower of the tank in which he recognized that 'the worst obstacle to the tank is the landmine, possibilities of which have yet to be fully developed.' Building on Liddell Hart's doctrine, Captain R.H. Dewing, Royal Engineers, provided a remarkably prescient description of mine warfare:

There will be little doubt that, in the event of our being engaged in a war against an enemy armed with tanks, there will be an immediate and insistent demand for every possible form of anti tank protection. Mines alone can never provide efficient protection, any more than barbed wire alone can be protection against infantry ... Their value is

> two-fold (i) Their physical value, arising from the power of rendering tanks immobile, (ii) their moral value arising from the effect on the nerves of the driver of a tank of the knowledge that he may at any moment drive into a minefield ... Three methods of destroying minefields have been suggested: (i) by artillery fire. (ii) By providing tanks with a roller ... (iii) By a form of plough pushed ahead of a tank ... the necessity for every tank formation being preceded by mine sweeping tanks would ... handicap ... the tanks, which would itself justify the use of the mines.

The discussions about anti-tank warfare prompted the Royal Engineers to design an anti-tank mine in 1928. This was superior to the mines used on the Western Front ten years earlier, being a flat pear shape, made of steel, containing 4.5lb of TNT, fired by depressing a knob on top of the mine. Due to financial restraints it was never put into production. It was 1935 before a new design, made from a modified cake tin and known as the Mark 1 Contact Mine, was produced in small numbers.

It is no accident that in the mid 1930s the British started to consider the potential of the anti-tank mine with a degree of purpose. Tensions were being felt throughout Europe as a result of Hitler's rearmament, and the threat of another major war was building. The Germans tested a number of prototype tanks (or 'panzers' as they were known in German) and Guderian, one of the most prominent panzer generals of the war, was beginning to articulate his theory of mobile armoured warfare: 'Where tanks succeed, victory follows'. In 1935, the British held their first anti-tank exercise using three levels of simulated anti-tank minefield. The highest level contained 1,500 mines per 1,000 yards and offered 100 per cent protection from enemy tanks; the second, 1,000 mines per 1,000 yards with 80 per cent protection; and the third, 700 mines per 1,000 yards offering 50 per cent protection. But the 'suggestions that a Division would require five to six thousand mines across its front were met with incredulity if not ribaldry' by many officers for whom the concept of armoured warfare was entirely alien.

Anti-personnel mine development was neglected altogether in the inter-war period. They had been used by the British Army for decades, but there was no standard design and they had always been improvised in the field. The stone fougasse still appeared in military engineering manuals well into the 1930s and it was not until 1940 that any anti-personnel mines were mass produced.

Whilst the potential of anti-tank mines was beginning to be appreciated in some quarters, and a modest design had been produced in small numbers, the reality was that little had been achieved in practical terms by the outbreak of hostilities in 1939. Training, field trials and doctrine had been overlooked. Although the British Expeditionary Force had taken stocks of mines to Belgium and Northern France, it was considered inappropriate to lay these mines during the phoney war as farmers were still working the fields, and during the rapid retreat few mines were used for their designed purpose, many being used as bridge demolition charges. Brigadier Young, writing of the British Army's retreat in 1940, observed: 'Looking back now it seems ludicrous and certainly pathetic ... that mines were never used. There were many reasons why, but basically there were few mines and the soldiers had never seen one, let alone trained on them.' The American experience was little different, with an official report claiming that 'mine warfare was perhaps the most serious training deficit. The pre-war army failed to anticipate the importance of mines and booby traps.' Indeed, one American officer claimed that he 'had never seen a German mine, picture or model before entering combat'.

The French put their faith in the static defences of the Maginot Line to resist a German attack. This was a line of concrete fortifications and machine-gun posts along their Eastern border. After the invasion of Poland they developed two anti-tank mines, an anti-personnel mine and a series of pressure and time-delay fuses adapted for use in artillery shells (as the Germans had done in the First World War). Large stocks of these mines were captured by the Germans and used when the Allies invaded France four years later.[2]

The Germans had spent the later months of the First World War on the back foot, resisting massed tank attacks, and had appreciated the potential of mines as defensive weapons. In the inter-war period they produced two effective anti-tank mines and one highly innovative anti-personnel mine, so they were a step ahead of the Allies at the outbreak of war. Their first anti-tank mine, the

Tellermine 29 (in English: the plate mine; the figure relates to the year of manufacture)[3] was produced in 1929. This was upgraded in 1935 as the *Tellermine 35*,[4] which had a more efficient pressure fuse and a larger charge weight. A testament to their durability was that they remained in production in Yugoslavia until the 1980s.

In 1940, French troops skirmishing between the Maginot and Siegfried lines (along the Franco–German border) encountered a device which bounded out of the ground and detonated at waist height spraying thousands of steel balls in all directions. They had discovered the German *Schrapnell Mine 35*, or as Allied soldiers called it, the S Mine. This was not an entirely new idea. The US military had designed what they called a 'shell fougasse' in the 1850s, and a Norwegian engineer had published an article in the *Scientific American* in 1916 describing a 'mine grenade', both of which were essentially bounding fragmentation mines. What was new about the S mine was that it combined maximum destructive power in a small, easily concealed format with three initiation options (pressure, tripwire or electrical). Shrapnel technology had been around since the early nineteenth century when Henry Shrapnel, a British artillery officer, established that the force of an explosion could launch small steel fragments at high velocity, creating a much more lethal effect than ordinary explosive blast. In the First World War shrapnel shells were used by the thousand to kill infantry in the open. The S mine acted like a shrapnel shell, but it did not need an artillery piece to fire it; it had pinpoint accuracy, could be initiated either by enemy troops or on command, and the maximum spread of shrapnel was achieved as it detonated above ground. The Germans produced over 9 million of this highly efficient mine and it soon became one of the most feared weapons of the war.

With the incorporation of high explosives into mines, they became more reliable and more powerful. This was the technical breakthrough that allowed mines to proliferate. But it was several decades after the invention of high explosives before they were used in significant numbers. The catalyst for modern mine warfare was the introduction of the tank. It was not a clash of equals – indeed the tank and the mine represent the antithesis of each other. A tank has a crew, it is expensive, mobile, armoured, a proud statement of military virility. A mine is unmanned, concealed, cheap, invidious and inglorious. But neutralizing the tank was often much easier than neutralizing the mine.

Notes

1 This is quoted in Byron Farwell's *The Great War in Africa* (London, Norton, 1986). It seems more probable that the pipe was wider than a quarter of an inch – perhaps three quarters or a full inch.

2 I was asked to clear a field about half the size of a football pitch in Cambodia that had been grazed by cattle. There were hoof prints over every square inch of the field. The villagers insisted that mines remained in it, but I was convinced that any mines would have been initiated by the cattle. I was astonished to find eight mines in the field, four of them fully functioning. I have remained skeptical about the wisdom of 'cattle clearance' ever since.

3 The Germans gave them a nomenclature of their own: the heavy anti-tank mine became the PzMi 420(f) and the light anti-tank mine PzMi 407(f). PzMi means *Panzerabwehrmine* which translates as 'anti-tank mine'. The anti-personnel mine was the *Sprengen Mine 442* (f) – jumping mine.

4 The *Tellermine 29* had three separate, button-like pressure fuses and a TNT charge of 4kg.

5 German mine nomenclature follows a logical sequence. Conventional anti-tank (AT) mines were known as *Tellerminen* (plate mines in English), often using abbreviations, so a *Tellermine 35* was a T.Mi.35. The figure after the letter usually refers to the year of design. Anti-personnel (AP) mines were known by their effect, so *Schrapnell Mine 35* (S.Mi.35) literally does what it says on the tin.

Chapter 4

A New Arm of Warfare

—m—

*No matter how slowly or methodically mine clearance
teams worked, they could never guarantee a clear route.*
US Lieutenant Colonel Davis, Tunisia, 1943

B y the start of the Second World War, a variety of mines had
been used across the world for several hundred years, several
thousand years if we include their spiked antecedents. Mines
had incorporated new technology as it had become available and had
gradually become more effective. Although there had been some
reservations about the ethics of using these unchivalrous, largely
unseen, victim-operated weapons, these were soon brushed aside.
The mine had hitherto remained a peripheral weapon but this
changed very rapidly during the Second World War when a heavy
reliance on mines produced what the American General McNair saw
as 'a new arm of warfare'.

Employing blitzkrieg tactics the Germans advanced rapidly on all
fronts until 1942 when they were overextended in North Africa.
From then on the Germans fought the war on the defensive and they
placed an increasing significance on the use of landmines as an
attritional weapon. The shift from an offensive to a defensive posture
is starkly seen in German mine production figures which increased
sharply after 1942.

Year	1939	1940	1941	1942	1943	1944	1945
Mine Production (millions)	2.5	3.2	3.0	8.6	21.5	41.5	9.5

These figures mask a very significant trend; there was an increase, not only of numbers of mines, but also in the numbers of different types of mines. The Germans started the war with two anti-tank and one anti-personnel mine. By 1945 they had developed sixteen different types of anti-tank mine and ten different types of anti-personnel mine, and used dozens of types of captured mines. The majority of German mines were not minor modifications or cosmetic differences, but entirely new devices incorporating new operating principles and new materials to fulfil new tactical requirements. The key reason to introduce new types of mine was the need to stay ahead of the range of mine countermeasures deployed by the Allies.

The duel between mine and mine countermeasures had a dramatic opening stage along the fringes of the Sahara Desert in North Africa. The vast, flat expanse of sand and rock was almost featureless and landmines offered one of the few means of protection. In stark contrast to the static trench warfare of 1914–1918, the age of mobile armoured warfare had arrived and combat in North Africa was very fluid with most troops moving not on foot, but by vehicles. To defend their positions both sides laid hundreds of thousands of anti-tank mines. The pace of combat was so rapid that attempts were made to breach minefields a few days or weeks after they were laid. Recently disturbed sand gave away the locations of buried anti-tank mines, and as they needed a pressure of around 150kg to initiate them, they could be located and removed with relative ease.

To prevent the lifting and subsequent relaying of minefields, a common practice at the beginning of the war, the Germans seeded their anti-tank minefields with the deadly new S mine and fitted anti-tank mines with anti-lifting devices, small fuzes that screwed into the side or the base of a mine that would cause it to detonate if moved. From around 1941 around 3 per cent of all anti-tank mines were fitted with them. As it was impossible to tell, without painstaking excavation, which mines were fitted with anti-lifting devices, every mine located had to be pulled from the ground using a long rope. If it was connected to an anti-lifting device the mine would detonate. The combination of the S mine and the anti-lift device made mine clearing very much more difficult, especially as mine-clearing operations were often conducted at night when disturbed ground was difficult to spot. The countermeasure was to prod for mines using a bayonet or sharp stick which, to be effective, needed to be done in a formal pattern. To locate a German 30cm diameter *Tellermine* a prodder had to be inserted into the earth at a 30° angle from the horizontal (to avoid direct pressure on the pressure plate) every 20cm. So to clear one square metre a prodder had to be inserted twenty-five times (five times across a one metre lane repeated five times at 20cm intervals into the lane). Add the possibility of buried S mines, which were 10cm in diameter, and to guarantee locating them in a one-metre square, the prodder had to be inserted every 7 or 8cm, or over 150 times a square metre.[1] The task was not purely mathematical – soldiers were under the constant threat of being blown up by a mine whilst prodding, or being shot at by the enemy. So an unusual combination of diligence, patience and raw courage was demanded of mine clearers.

All mines at the beginning of the war used metal for their casing, pressure plates and fuzes. That metal might be located using some form of electronic detectors had been established some years earlier by Alexander Graham Bell, the inventor of the telephone. Legend relates that in 1881, when US President James Garfield was lying fatally wounded by an assassin's bullet, Bell attempted to locate the bullet using his prototype metal detector. The attempt was unsuccessful as the metal bed springs interfered with his detector. At the first threat of invasion Britain had hastily mined many beaches around southern and eastern Britain (described in greater detail in Chapter 6). The requirement to remove or relay some of these mines had highlighted the need for a rapid method of locating mines and the War Office issued a specification for a metal detector. In Poland during the 1930s a need arose to locate unexploded shells on artillery training grounds and some work had progressed in this area. At the

Electronic mine detectors were introduced early in the war, but locating mines remained slow and dangerous, frequently delaying advancing forces.

outbreak of war many Poles fled to England including Lieutenant Józef Kosacki, who submitted the successful design, based partially on the earlier work in Poland. The Polish detector had two coils, one of which was connected to an oscillator which generated an oscillating current of an acoustic frequency. The other coil was connected to an amplifier and a telephone. When the coils came into proximity with a metallic object the balance between them was upset and it made an audible signal. The equipment weighed just under 30lb (14 kg) and could be operated by one man. The detector was produced by Cinema Television Ltd,[2] a company that specialized in televisions but was engaged in a variety of high-technology, war-related production including radar display tubes. Thousands of Polish mine detectors were produced; the last variant, the 4C, saw service in the 1991 Gulf War.

The Americans, Germans and Russians produced mine detectors early in the war and they soon proved their utility by increasing the speed at which mines could be located. The theory of using a detector was quite simple – it would be passed over the ground until a signal indicated the presence of metal. The area would be investigated using a prodder and if a mine was located it could be disarmed or destroyed. However the practice remained slow. The detectors would signal the presence of not just mines but any metal, including discarded nuts and bolts, shrapnel and old bullets. This often meant dozens of signals would have to be investigated before a mine was located. The planning speed to breach a one-metre-wide lane through a minefield, using a party of up to six men, was one metre per minute, but it could be much slower.

An effective way of retarding the already slow breaching process was to make minefields wider. In 1918, the Germans started to take a scientific approach to laying minefields; by 1942 this had crystallized into a formal doctrine and was embedded throughout their field forces. As a British officer put it: 'No one who had first-hand experience of following up a German retreat can forget the thoroughness of their [mine laying] methods.' Three basic types of minefields were used: defensive, in front of field units and often very large; nuisance, along lines of communication, bridges or areas likely to be occupied by the enemy; and dummy, which had the appearance of a real minefield but did not contain mines. Minefields were integrated into an overall defensive plan and surveyed in great detail, down to the position of individual mines. To ensure that mines could be located after they had outlived their tactic usefulness, a series of reference points were carefully plotted and marked on the ground using steel bars set in concrete. Lifting their own minefields was not a humanitarian gesture, but in the wartime world of scare resources, and in areas where counter-attacks might be necessary, was a highly practical consideration.

Mines were laid in uniform patterns using a measuring wire with markers along it, indicating the point at which mines should be laid. In tactical minefields up to sixteen rows of mines were laid; these would be offset to ensure the maximum chance that a tank would be hit. Laying mines was choreographed into a rigid drill. Fifty men each carrying four mines (German anti-tank mines were fitted with handles) were lined up on the measuring wires at the markers. On command they would lay a mine at their feet. The whole line then advanced six paces, turned left, advanced three paces and laid another mine. The process was repeated with the other two mines. The whole line then returned to bury, arm (by inserting a fuze or detonator) and camouflage the mine. In favourable conditions a minefield 300m long by 18m wide, containing 200 mines, could be laid in forty-five minutes. Standard minefields could contain up to sixteen rows of mines in depths of up to 100m. Gaps with no mines (known as safe lanes) were incorporated to allow counter-attacks through the minefield. Anti-personnel mines, some with tripwires, were laid amongst the anti-tank mines along its forward edge. The Germans kept detailed records on standard reporting forms. They also placed a heavy emphasis on ensuring that minefields could easily be located by friendly forces using a series of standard warning signs. The enemy side might be unmarked or have a single strand of barbed wire with a red warning triangle with the words 'Achtung Minen'. German minefields were guarded, often extensively, and covered by both artillery and machine-gun fire. Minefields were therefore highly effective obstacles and clearing them was no easy task.

Breaching minefields with a mine detector might have been somewhat quicker than prodding, but crossing a field 100m wide still took two hours – unless the breaching party was attacked in which progress might be impossible. Attacking tanks wanted to use their armour, mobility and firepower to spearhead a rapid advance rather than creep forward behind soldiers slowly picking their way through minefields, detectors in hand, or 'handmaids with hoovers' as they were sometimes ungratefully called. Yet the attacking thrust of a tank formation could quickly founder when their tracks were blown off by mines. Moreover, immobilized tanks were vulnerable to direct fire weapons, yet if crews attempted to escape on foot they were prey to anti-personnel mines. It was with this conundrum in mind that the word 'minefield' entered the lexicon, meaning a situation beset with problems.

Locating minefields in advance of an attack was clearly essential. Aerial reconnaissance was one option that yielded useful information on the location of minefields especially in the desert. Once minefields were identified the problem of breaching them started. Throughout the war attempts were made to use aerial or artillery bombardment to create safe areas, but the results were never entirely satisfactory. Aerial bombs could not be dropped with sufficient accuracy and large bombs left sizeable craters making the terrain difficult for tanks.[3] At Omaha Beach on D-Day, US troops were told that most mines would be cleared by aerial bombardment and were surprised to discover, as one GI put it: 'no craters on the beach, but plenty of mines everywhere'. Artillery was more promising, but there were still problems with accuracy and cratering of the ground.[4] The British adapted an anti-submarine system known as the 'hedgehog' for breaching beach minefields in advance of a seaborne assault. This was an array of twenty-four spigot mortar depth charges mounted in a small, specially strengthened assault boat. The boat would approach a mined beach and fire all the charges which had a high trajectory and fell in a tight pattern 120m long and 8m wide just 100m in front of the boat, destroying mines in its path. The theory was sound but in practice was disappointing. During the Allied landings at Salerno in 1943 two hedgehogs were used, but they landed along the edge of the minefield and killed several soldiers. They had however shown sufficient potential to be used to breach some minefields in advance of the British D-Day landings. Based at Hamble in the South of England, they were organized into flotillas and the dangerous nature of their task earned them the nickname 'The Crazy Gang'. The small craft were towed across the Channel by larger ships and planned to motor to their positions once they were within a few miles of the French coast. In the unexpectedly rough seas, twenty of the small craft sank under tow as there was no provision for slipping the tow ropes once the convoy was under way. However, twenty-one craft fired their hedgehogs which the commander of 69 Infantry Brigade claimed provided 'invaluable work in getting my men ashore safely'. In general, though, clearance by bombardment was highly inefficient and mines were often redistributed rather than destroyed, so it was rarely an attractive option.

At the end of the First World War trials had been conducted with tanks fitted with heavy rollers to detonate mines ahead of the tracks and the British tried these again in North Africa. As the first designs of rollers could not survive multiple mine detonations the concept was changed to a 'pilot vehicle'. This was a cargo truck with an armoured cab that pushed concrete rollers with embedded steel spikes, and was designed to be driven at the head of an advancing column to indicate the beginning of a minefield by detonating the first mine encountered. It would then reverse leaving what remained of the rollers, and allow men with detectors and prodders to complete the task. The *Tactical Employment Handbook* stated: 'Pilot vehicles are one-shot vehicles. Drivers of pilot vehicles are subject to considerable strain of a peculiar nature.'

As the war progressed stronger rollers were developed that were fitted to tanks. However, problems with their durability remained – repeated mine detonations would render them unserviceable, they only cleared the width of a tank's tracks and their weight greatly restricted a tank's mobility. An American divisional commander described tanks fitted with rollers as 'the most effective roadblock his troops encountered in Europe'.

The problem of countermine equipment being destroyed on the first row of mines could be countered by using a plough instead of rollers. This heavy pronged device was fitted in front of tank tracks and ploughed the earth to a depth of around 30cm, pushing aside any buried mines ahead of it. Like rollers it restricted a tank's mobility, cleared only a narrow path and many of the tanks of the Second World War lacked the power to push it through hard soil. Armoured bulldozers proved a useful alternative, with a better weight-to-power ration and capable of ploughing the full width of a vehicle; they were frequently used as an expedient clearance method. The dozer blade pushed aside the topsoil where mines were planted leaving a clear path for following troops. Operators wore 'flak suits' to protect against S mines, but even so it was a terrifying occupation. An after-action report claimed that: 'More than fifty American bulldozers struck mines during the campaign for Italy. In many cases operators were thrown from their seats, but none were killed. Some had broken legs, but had they been in cabs with roofs many would have had their necks broken or skulls fractured.'

Locating mines using a metal detector, whilst not without its limitations, was reasonably effective at the beginning of the war when mines contained a large amount of metal. A Polish mine detector could locate a buried *Tellermine* at up to 50cm depth. To make the job more difficult for detector teams, metal scrap would be scattered around mined areas or mines would be buried under a stout wooden pole, too deep to be detected, but a vehicle could still apply sufficient pressure through the pole to detonate the mine. A more enduring response was to reduce the metal content of mines to make them undetectable. Throughout the war and the second half of the twentieth century there was a battle between mines with ever smaller amounts of metal, and metal detectors that were increasingly sensitive. In 1942, the Germans introduced anti-personnel (*Schutzen Mine 42* or *schu* mine) and anti-tank mines (*Holzmine 42*) with wooden casings.[5] Both had metal fuses, but were practically undetectable using early metal detectors. The Germans produced 20 million *schu* mines during the war, (which were widely copied and remained in common use in many countries until the end of the twentieth century). The *schu* mine proliferated because it was highly effective, cheap and easy to make. It was a small pressure-operated mine built around a standard 200–gram explosive charge, which could blow off a man's foot, ankle and lower leg. Although serious and requiring significant medical treatment, amputations of this nature are survivable. In an attritional war the equation was highly effective – one man would be taken out of battle permanently, requiring at least two men to carry him to a dressing station. He would then need extensive medical treatment and repatriation, further draining resources and eroding the morale of other soldiers at the front and civilians at home. Other weapons kill or injure, but none are deliberately designed to disfigure in this way. The *schu* mine was the most common mine in the Second World War but it was not the only minimum-metal, pressure-operated mine. In 1940 the Russians produced a small round mine with a pressed cardboard casing and containing 90 grams of explosive which was known as the PMK40.[6] The Italians, one of the great innovators of mine technology, developed an anti-tank mine in Pignone in north-west Italy, made from bakelite, a form of plastic used to make early telephone sets, cameras and used as casings in a number of later Warsaw Pact mines. Experience of encountering Russian minimum-metal mines on the Eastern front prompted the Germans to develop their own.

German minimum-metal mines served a double purpose: they were very difficult to detect and they did not deplete Germany's dwindling supplies of steel upon which the war was making great demands. As well as wood, mine casings were made from glass, concrete and clay. In 1943, Hitler demanded that his weapons designers went a step further. 'The other day I was thinking about if it wouldn't be possible to infest the minefields with other mines, as well as anti-personnel mines, to such an extent that even our own men can't pass through [them], because they explode no matter who steps on them. These mines should be cased in plastic instead of metal.' His demands were met in 1944 in the form of an anti-tank mine known as the *Topfmine 4531* that was entirely without metal parts. The *Topfmine* had several different types of casing including mixtures of sawdust, tar, coal and bitumen. It contained a glass ampoule with a chemical mixture that detonated the 10kg main charge on receiving a pressure of around 150kg. From 1944 onwards they were encountered in great numbers in North-West Europe. The Americans remarked that 'particularly disturbing were the nests of non-metallic anti-personnel *schu* mines and anti-tank *Topfmines*, neither of which respond to ordinary mine detectors.' The *Topfmine* did however respond to the German *Stuttgart 43* detector. The Allies were aware that the Germans were capable of locating buried *Topfmines* but were uncertain how they achieved this. They noticed that each buried mine was surrounded by a small quantity of sand and assumed that the *Stuttgart 43* identified a special property within the sand, pouches of which were issued with each mine. It was not until after the war that they passed a Geiger counter over the sand and the secret was discovered: the sand, known to the Germans as *Tarnsand*,[7] was radioactive.

The German's desire to economize on materials and increase the efficiency of minefields led them to develop a mine in a new format. Conventional mines were about 30cm in diameter and it was literally a case of hit or miss for a tank's tracks to pass over it. Increasing the size of the mine would increase its chance of being hit by a tank and reduce the numbers of mines needed in a minefield. The Italians had considered this factor when developing their B2 and V3 mines which they used in Africa in the first months of the war. These were 80cm long and 10cm wide, making them nearly three times as likely to be hit by a mine. They had metal casings so they were easy to locate using metal detectors, but they reduced the numbers of mines needed in a minefield with consequent savings in manufacturing, logistics loads and time needed to lay a minefield. The German version was known as the *Riegelmine 43* and nearly 3 million were produced towards the end of the year.

The search for effective mine countermeasures continued apace. Clearance using aerial and artillery bombardment proved disappointing but the principle was sound enough: detonate sufficient explosive on or close to landmines and they will be destroyed or may sympathetically detonate. It was the application of the explosive that proved difficult. Some inspiration came in the form of the Bangalore torpedo which was invented in India in 1912. This was a long thin tube, filled with explosives, designed to clear barbed wire. Soldiers found that if pushed into a minefield and detonated it also cleared mines along its path. But it was too short for most minefields and contained insufficient explosive to clear a wide path, so the next step was to build a very large Bangalore torpedo. This development was taken forward by the Canadian Army in the form of the Snake. The Snake was a series of tubes 76mm in diameter and about 6m long, containing explosive. It was originally invented to be fitted to a tank and fired length by length into a minefield just ahead of the tank. The rocket mechanism designed to propel the tubes into the minefield proved unreliable so lengths of Snake were joined together and shunted forward. It was first used in action at Le Havre in 1944. The successor to the Snake was the Conger – 300m of flexible hose 5cm in diameter – that was fired across a minefield by a rocket and then pumped full of liquid nitroglycerine and detonated. Liquid nitroglycerine was just as unstable as it was in the 1860s and it was withdrawn from service after a dramatic accident in Holland in

October 1944 involving 248 Armoured Assault Squadron, Royal Engineers, near the village of Ijzendijke. The nitroglycerine detonated whilst being unloaded, killing twenty-six British and fifteen Canadian soldiers, and wounding forty-three others. A memorial to commemorate the loss was unveiled on the site in 1997.

The Allies, conscious of the effects of explosive clearance, designed mines to counter this method. No mine could survive close contact with a heavy explosive hose, but if the mine's pressure plate was simply replaced with an X-shaped metal grid, it could withstand considerable blast pressure whilst retaining the ability to initiate under a tank's tracks.[8] Explosive clearance methods never fulfilled their potential and did not concern the Germans sufficiently for them to develop blast-resistant mines of their own.

The potential of rollers and ploughs did, however, concern the Germans, as did the limitations of the pressure-operated anti-tank mine, which simply shattered a tank's tracks leaving it immobile. In a well-defended minefield the tank was vulnerable to direct fire, but it would be preferable to totally destroy a tank to prevent it from being repaired and reused. *Tellermines* were sometimes fitted with vertical rods that were designed to be struck by a tank's hull. The rod ensured that the mine could be initiated by the full width of the tank, rather than just the tracks. But destroying an armour-plated tank was not easy – explosive needs to be in close contact with armour in order to cut it. A tank could withstand a nearby blast, and even increasing the explosive charge weight or planting double mines was not entirely successful. Having increased the initiation rate of anti tank mines, the next stage of the evolution was to increase a mine's destructive capability. A solution came in the form of the Monroe Effect, or shaped charge. Named after its discoverer, Charles Monroe, a scientist at the US Naval Torpedo Station in Newport in 1888, who discovered that when explosive is detonated, the shock waves move at great speed from the point of initiation and that these shock waves could be focussed. If a conical hole is made in a cylinder of explosive and lined with metal at one end, initiation from the opposite end causes the shock wave to travel along the axis of the cylinder inverting the metal liner, which forms a focused plasma jet capable of punching through great thickness of armour. The shaped charge was used in anti-tank rockets that started to appear early in the war, such as the US bazooka, Russian RPG and the German *Panzerfaust*. Combining the tilt rod with a shaped charge proved an efficient solution in the form of the *Hohlladungs-Springmine* and its smaller cousin the *Panzer Stab Mine*.[9] A tank's hull would strike the tilt rod which initiated the mine sending its plasma jet through the belly of the tank, destroying it and killing the crew. It was used in small numbers towards the end of the war.

The Russians developed an unusual type of mine that could attack the full width of a tank. Dogs were trained to associate the underside of tanks with food. They were fitted with a canvas back-pack containing 12kg of TNT on either side, on short delay timers. The original concept was for the dog to run under the tank and, on hearing a whistle blast from its handler, bite a lever protruding from its collar that would drop the charges, before running back to its handler as the tank was blown up. This could only work at close range on static tanks, so the lever was swapped for a wooden tilt rod that protruded from the dog's back which detonated the charge as the dog ran underneath the tank. This was more workable but these canine kamikaze missions demanded a much larger pool of trained dogs. A unit of thirty dogs was operational against the Germans in summer 1941. Its commander, Captain Viporasskogo, reported in October 1941 that most dogs' instinct for self-preservation was greater than their hunger and they jumped for cover at the first sound of gunfire, endangering all around them. Three dogs were shot before they reached their targets by the German troops as they advanced, and four tanks exploded when being attacked by dog mines, but it was not clear if mines, anti-tank fire or the dogs were responsible. Further training was needed to refine the concept but the tanks and the fuel could not be spared so by 1942 it was decided to cease the dog mine operation. It remains one of the strangest episodes in the history of the mine.

As well as dog mines there were also mine dogs. In 1940, the British established a school to explore the potential of dogs to assist with guarding, patrolling and delivering messages. As the challenges of detecting minimum-metal mines mounted, experiments were conducted to see if dogs might provide a solution – dogs were trained to associate the smell of buried mines with food. A journalist from *The Times* observing a mine dogs' display wrote: 'No one seems to know yet what sense comes into play ... but long experience of finding buried bones may have something to do with it.' In June 1944, four dog platoons were deployed to North-West Europe with the British and Canadian invading forces. Their survival instinct was, like the Russian dog mines, stronger than their appetite and they could not be used to locate front-line minefields under fire. They did however prove their worth away from the fighting and did some valuable work clearing roads and railway lines. They located relatively few mines, but the commander of one of the dog platoons put this in perspective, explaining that:

> The value of the mine clearing dog cannot be assessed by the number of mines located with his aid ... his real value ... was the saving of time and labour, and in the saving of lives of both soldiers and civilians. Quite incidentally in the course of his daily duties he found very few mines over areas which, but for his aid, might have remained unchecked for a long time, used at great risk, or else unused at great economic cost.

So their value was not just in locating mines, but confirming that areas were clear of landmines, and this they could do very much faster than a man with a detector.

Dogs had a role to play in detecting mines, but the problem of rapidly clearing a breach through a defended minefield remained. It was clear that a mechanized approach was needed. Tanks equipped with rollers or ploughs offered a partial solution but they were difficult to push and created very narrow lanes. A faster, more manoeuvrable and more thorough option was the flail tank, whose pioneers were mostly South African engineers. The flail was a series of chains attached to a rapidly rotating cylinder mounted on a moveable boom on the front of a tank. The chains spun with the cylinder and beat the ground in front of the tank detonating or disrupting the mines it encountered. The first operational flail tank, known as the Scorpion, was based on the British Matilda tank and appeared in the North African desert in 1942. The Matilda had a second engine fitted in an armoured box mounted on the side of the tank which included a space for a crewman who operated the device. Twenty-five Scorpions were deployed to breach German minefields during the Second Battle of El Alamein with somewhat mixed results. They churned up such vast quantities of sand and dust that the crew needed to wear gas masks and it obscured the battlefield like the gunpowder smoke of the Napoleonic era. This made it difficult for the crew to see where they were going, but concealed them from German gunners. Whilst they cleared some mines, others were hurled in all directions, some detonating against the tank. The flails' constant height could not cope with small depressions and mines at the bottom of these were untouched. And whilst they were faster than a party of engineers with detectors, their flailing speed was only one kilometre an hour, so they were hardly the vanguard of lightning attack. They did have an unexpected psychological effect: an Italian prisoner thought the 'slowly advancing pillar of dust, out of which came dreadful noises of clanking, grinding and rattling of chains, was more frightening than the artillery'.

Despite their limitations, flail tanks offered the best minefield breaching option of the war. Flails were fitted to the Sherman, one of the most successful Allied tanks of the war, and was known as the Crab, with over 300 ordered for the invasion of Europe. They provided a crucial service on D-Day and throughout the North-West Europe campaign where three Crabs often advanced in echelon to clear a broad path through minefields. The Crab was faster than the Scorpion, although at 2 kph this was still slow; they continued to miss some mines and redistribute others. It was an expedient solution – breaching minefields always costs time and lives, and forces investment in countermeasures equipment and training, which adds to the cost of making war.

From this account of mine and mine countermeasures development during the Second World War it may be assumed that each advance in mine technology was neatly followed by an advance in mine countermeasures technology, but this was not the case. The Second World War was fought on at least six major fronts, by many armies using a variety of different mines and mine countermeasures. Advances in mine warfare were neither universal nor incremental, although the general trends were clear enough. Paradoxically, one of the most significant advances in mine technology, the introduction of air-dropped scatterable mines, occurred at the start of the war, although its importance was underestimated at the time. The Germans used a system known as the *Sprengbombe Dickwandig* 2 kg or SD 2, and the Italians used the AR4, which was known to Allied troops as the Thermos bomb on account of its shape. The SD 2 was packed in containers and dropped en masse over a target, so they landed over a wide area. It was fitted with different types of fuses that either detonated on impact, after a delay of between five and thirty minutes, or if it was moved. The bombs contained 225 grams of TNT and could be lethal to anyone within a radius of 25m. They were dropped on Grimsby and Cleethorpes in England.

The thermos bomb was larger, containing around 600 grams of explosive and as the British Military Intelligence Service noted, it was 'designed to arm after it has come to rest on the ground. It is therefore in some respects an anti-personnel mine.' The Thermos bomb was dropped on North Africa and Malta. These scatterable systems did not have the dramatic effect of large bombs, with their massive blast waves spreading from the point of detonation, flattening trees and buildings. Scatterable systems not only cause immediate damage, they then paralyse large areas for days or weeks, causing damage, inflicting casualties and continuing disruption. The Germans and Italians did not appreciate the full impact of these weapons and they were rarely used. Their effectiveness was clear enough to the Americans who copied the SD2 after the war and dropped them in great numbers in Vietnam. The scatterable mine system was developed further in the 1970s and they became an important weapon in many countries' arsenals in the late twentieth century.

Notes

1 In 1942 the British introduced a ground spike mine that fired a bullet vertically when trodden on. It had a diameter of around 3cm.

2 Cinema Television Ltd was formed in 1939 from John Logie Baird's (the inventor of the television) company Baird TV, and became part of the Rank Organisation in 1958.

3 Explosive clearance of minefields using aerial bombardment was tested in 1944 by the Americans on military reserves in Florida and Virginia. Nine B-17 and nine B-29 aircraft each dropped ten 350lb Mark 47 bombs (i.e. 180 bombs in total) from between 8,500 and 7,600ft. The result was a breach 55ft wide across the 300ft deep minefield. Rates of clearance were: 100 per cent of *Tellermines*, 95 per cent of *schu* mines and 76 per cent of S mines. The conclusion was that whilst is was possible to breach a minefield using air-dropped bombs, the execution was technically difficult and the results were unsatisfactory, as they left mines uncleared and the cratered ground was difficult to cross

4 The Russians often attempted clearance by bombardment. It was standard practice to fire 500 rounds of 76mm shells to breach a lane 8m wide and 100m long.

5 The Finns used wooden box mines during the Winter War of 1939. Their choice of material was dictated by availability rather than concerns about ease of detection.

6 In the early 1960s the PMK40 was replaced by the PMN which was made of Bakelite and contained 240grams of explosives. The Soviets also manufactured their own version of the schu mine which they designated the PMD40. Together they were the most commonly encountered anti-personnel mines of the late twentieth century.

7 *Tarnsand* was better known as Thorium, a commonly occurring, radioactive, non-fissile material (i.e. not capable of sustaining a chain reaction of nuclear fission). It is found in many parts of the world including Norway – the German's probable source.

8 This simple countermeasure was fitted to the British Mark V and American M 4 anti-tank mines.

9 At the time the *Hohlladungs-Springmine* or *HL.Sp.Mi. 4672* ('hollow-charge jump mine') and the *Panzer Stab Mine* or *Pz Stab. Mi 43* were introduced there was great competition for scarce resources and many felt it better to use the warheads for the proven *Panzerfaust* rockets rather than an untried new weapon.

Chapter 5

The Second World War: Mines on the Battlefield

—⟋⟋⟍—

Often the sole obstacle that could be established.
Basil Liddell Hart

During the Second World War there were rapid advances in mine technology and in countermeasures designed to defeat mines, with both locked in a continuous struggle for supremacy. But the key determinant of how many mines were used, and where they were laid, was terrain. Mines were laid specifically to create an obstacle to defend against armoured attack, so they were laid on 'tankable' ground – ground that tanks could traverse. The more open the ground, the more mines were laid. Featureless deserts such as North Africa, or open steppe such as Eastern Europe, therefore needed millions of mines to create defensive lines, but mountainous regions such as central Italy, or dense jungle such as Burma, where tank movement was restricted, required few mines to block key routes.

In the First World War less than ten thousand tanks were used compared with about a quarter of a million in the Second World War. This massive increase was reflected in mine use which leapt from a few thousand during the First World War to tens of millions in the Second. In some ways mines were like all obstacles used by defenders – they could block, channel or delay an attacker's advance.

Anti-tank ditches, wire entanglements, concrete tank traps and other obstacles can influence an attacker's courses of action. But mines also have the ability to directly inflict casualties and, as they are unseen, they create fear and uncertainty, and the countermeasures needed to breach a minefield are varied and rarely immediately obvious. Mines have an innate attritional function which can grind down offensive capability making them disproportionately more effective than other obstacles.

The first mines of the Second World War were laid by the Finns to defend against Soviet invaders who attacked with overwhelming force in November 1939, in what became known as the Winter War. Finland's lengthy border with Russia was relatively flat, dotted with numerous lakes and covered with thick forest. Tankable terrain was therefore restricted to roads and tracks that criss-crossed the forests in the border region. The Finns had only 250,000 men and thirty tanks compared with the Soviets one million men and over 6,000 tanks. To resist invasion they had built what they termed the Mannerheim Line.[1] This was a line of machine-gun and artillery emplacements stretching from the Gulf of Finland to Lake Ladoga (the large lake on the eastern flank of the approaches to southern Finland). The Mannerheim Line integrated its fortifications with lakes and forests, and used mines to enhance the natural defences. Tankable ground was mined using a density of one or two anti-tank mines per metre of front. Roads and tracks were mined using a density of ten to fifty anti-tank mines per road kilometre.[2] By 1939, Finland had developed two effective anti-tank mines supplemented by two more types hurriedly improvised from wood at the start of the war.

The Finns' defended vigorously taking 70,000 casualties but inflicting massive losses on the Soviets who lost perhaps 400,000 dead and wounded, and over 2,200 tanks. The Soviets aimed to occupy the whole of Finland but the stout resistance persuaded them otherwise and in March 1940 they sued for peace on lesser terms.

The integration of mines into a robust overall defensive plan was a major factor in slowing down a much larger force, enabling the Finns to transform tankable terrain into killing zones for Soviet tanks. The success was to have lasting importance for both sides. The Soviets used Finnish mining tactics to slow down the German invasion of Russia in 1942; they also copied and manufactured millions of wooden mines which were virtually undetectable to wartime metal detectors. Perhaps the clearest indication of the effectiveness of mines in the Winter War is the fact that the Finns, in the face of considerable international pressure, remain one of the few Western countries who have not signed the landmine ban treaty.

The use of mobile armoured warfare in a largely featureless desert resulted in the North African campaign of 1940–1943 being described as 'dominated by the tank and the mine in circumstances that favoured the former and could only be overcome by prodigal expense of the latter'.[3] This was the campaign that defined and institutionalized mine warfare in modern military doctrine. Unlike in Finland, there were no natural defences to supplement, so they provided practically the only means of defence available from massed armoured attack. The campaign was conducted along a coastal strip around 80km wide along which ran the only main road. Seaports every few hundred kilometres provided the sole means of supply and marshes on the fringes of the open expanse of the Sahara restricted movement to the south. Furthermore the problem of supplying troops across the waterless desert meant that commanders sought economies in manpower through the massive use of field defences.

Recognizing the need for mines, and with supply lines stretching thousands of miles back to Britain across hazardous seaways, the British Army established mine factories in Egypt to manufacture what were called Egyptian Pattern (EP) anti-tank mines. Because of the difficulties of producing springs in Egypt, the first mine, the EP1, used a chemical fuze which was initiated by crushing a glass phial. No TNT was available for the main charge so dynamite, which was unstable in the heat, was used. The combination of the sensitive fuse and unstable explosive made them, in the words of a Royal Engineer officer, 'dangerous to lay and even more dangerous to lift' and production was stopped after 'many accidents in the hands of unskilled troops'. Egyptian Pattern mines went through six modifications in the first eighteen months of production in an effort to improve their operating mechanism and safety problems. Unlike the Germans, the British did not include a facility for anti-handling devices and they produced few anti-personnel mines, omissions that would have significant repercussions. Hundreds of thousands of mines were manufactured in a factory outside Cairo at a rate of 8,000 a day, using 2,400 Egyptian and Nigerian workers.

The North African campaign was a sequence of attacks and counter-attacks. In September 1940, the Italians attacked British-held Egypt but were quickly repulsed, and in December 1940, the British and their Allies advanced from Egypt into Italian-held Libya. After a series of defeats the Italians were reinforced by Rommel and his *Afrika Korps* in February 1941. In July 1942, the British were pushed back to Egypt where they succeeded in blunting Rommel's offensive. In November of the same year the Allies regained the offensive and, after being joined by US forces, succeeded in expelling Axis forces from North Africa in May 1943.

In September 1940, as they retreated from Egypt and Ethiopia, the Italians used anti-tank mines to delay the Allied advance. In Ethiopia, Second Lieutenant Premindra Singh Bhagat of the Indian Engineers led a detachment in the clearance of fifteen minefields along a 55-mile stretch of road, despite being ambushed and on two occasions having vehicles in which he was travelling blown up. The experience did him little harm. He was dispatched to New Delhi where he was awarded the Victoria Cross by the Viceroy and became a Lieutenant General before retiring.

In February 1941, the arrival of Rommel's *Afrika Korps* stopped the Allied advance at Gazala in Libya, where both sides used hundreds of thousands of mines to fortify their positions. Of the Allied defences Rommel wrote: 'The whole line had been planned with great skill ... countless numbers of mines have been laid – over one million in the Marmarica area alone.' At the time, it was by far the largest minefield ever laid. But size was no substitute for technique and the Allies demonstrated two key weaknesses. The first was that many of their minefields were not covered by direct fire, and the second, their minefields had no anti-personal mines or anti-lift devices. The operating pressure for anti-tank mines was greater than the weight of a man so German tank crews were able to dismount and clear lanes in front of their tanks. This, combined with superior strength and clever tactics, eventually overwhelmed the Allies who were forced to retreat, clearing many of their own mines for reuse as they went. They fell back around 150km to make a stand in what would be their final effort to protect Cairo and the Suez Canal, at a dusty railway junction called El Alamein.

At El Alamein, in July 1942, the Allies dug defensive positions supplemented by extensive minefields from the coast 60km inland to the Quattara Depression, whose isolated location and steep slopes made it impassable for tanks. Rommel's forces attacked the British position, but with supply lines overstretched and their forces outnumbered, they were ground down by an active defence. Tactically it was a stalemate, but strategically it was a victory for the Allies and in no small measure due to the attrition imposed by mines, which were integrated into the overall defence more efficiently than at Gazala.

Having lost the momentum of attack at El Alamein Rommel prepared a defensive line parallel to the Allies. By this time he had only 510 tanks against the Allies 1,350 and, with the Eastern Front sucking up vast amounts of German resources, he could expect no reinforcements. His best hope was to sow his front with as many mines as possible in the hope of wearing down any Allied attack, putting into practice the lessons learnt during the previous months. He ordered the creation of what became known as the 'Devil's Garden', a minefield so long and deep that it was considered virtually impenetrable when covered by artillery, small arms and the new and highly effective 88mm direct-fire guns. About 500,000 mines were laid in two parallel fields running north–south across the whole front with a total depth of about 5 miles. The bulk of the infantry and anti-tank guns were dug in inside the minefields. The tanks were positioned behind the minefields so they could provide a mobile reserve that could move to counter any attempted breakthrough.

The Allied attack on the German line was named Operation

Lightfoot in deference to the mines, and began on 23 October 1942. Engineers employing the new Polish mine detector and Scorpion flail tanks breached lanes in the minefields through which tanks could advance. But with so many mines laid in such deep minefields, the attack started to founder, as explained by Brigadier Roberts, commanding 22 Armoured Brigade:

> We tried for the first time to use what were called 'Scorpions' ... and they were very unreliable ... they broke down and got in the way and then the Sappers had to [clear the minefields] by hand – there was a great deal of delay. And after the first night we'd all got through what was the first minefield. And then we sat between the two minefields and [the Germans were] there ... absolutely looking down on us. It was a most uncomfortable situation. And then we tried again the next night ... and we went where the gap was and ... every tank was knocked out either by mines or anti tank fire. We struggled all night and made no progress. And so we called it off.

The mixed results of the flails meant that the brunt of mine-clearance duties fell to the Royal Engineers who advanced with 'deliberate, continuous sweeping with detectors, each man going forward slowly and intently, eyes on the ground, earphones on the head, while the noise of battle crashes around; and the cold blooded investigation and lifting of mines, never knowing when some heathenish invention for catching one out would not blow the grubber to eternity'.[4]

Over half of the Allies 1,100 tanks were lost at El Alamein, of which 20 per cent were caused by mines, with most of the remainder knocked out by direct-fire weapons inside minefields. But after twelve days of fighting the Germans were forced to retreat and the Allies won a decisive victory. In some ways the Second Battle of El Alamein was a mirror image of the First. So why did the Allies rather than the Germans succeed in holding and then breaking the line? Quite simply because the Allies had superior resources in both battles. Mines were important – they shaped the battle, dictating defensive positions and attacking formations, and they caused a significant stream of casualties. But the side with the greater resources was better able to withstand the attrition that they imposed.

North Africa was not the only campaign of the Second World War fought on open, tankable terrain. The 4 million square kilometres of the Great European Plain, devoid of mountains and significant forests, provided enormous scope for mobile armoured invaders. As in the desert, the defenders used vast quantities of mines.

Following the Winter War with Finland, the Soviets recognized the importance of mine warfare. By the time of the German invasion they had five anti-tank mines and two anti-personnel mines, and a clear sense of their importance in slowing down attackers. They organized at all tactical levels mobile obstacle detachments which laid tens of millions of mines during the war, supplemented by extensive tank ditches and infantry trenches that were often dug by civilians. They also placed a strong emphasis on laying mines during battles, often perilously close to approaching armour. By the end of the war the Soviets had around twenty types of anti-tank mines and six types of anti-personnel mines. Soviet mines lacked the precision engineering of their German counterparts but they exceeded their scale of production. Estimates of the numbers of mines used by the Soviets vary tremendously with some commentators suggesting a figure in excess of 200 million mines; a more credible source suggests 67 million. Whatever the true figure it was certainly prodigious. As the Russians put it: 'The invaders developed a great respect, at times even terror for the crafty, demon like use of mines that slowed down their advance and frequently stopped them completely.'

The campaign opened in June 1941 with a rapid German advance through Eastern Europe and into the USSR, where an early Russian winter and increasingly organized defence halted their progress at the gates of Moscow. In 1942, the Germans pushed south-east to Stalingrad and the trans-Caucasus before winter. In 1943, the USSR reversed some of the German gains and, in the climactic battle of the Eastern Front, the Germans attacked the Soviets at Kursk. By way of comparison El Alamein involved around 330,000 men and 1,600 tanks; Kursk involved 2.1 million men and 6,300 tanks.

At Kursk the Soviets prepared elaborate defences with eight defensive belts over a width of 35km. Each belt had an extensive network of trenches with interlocking artillery, machine-gun and

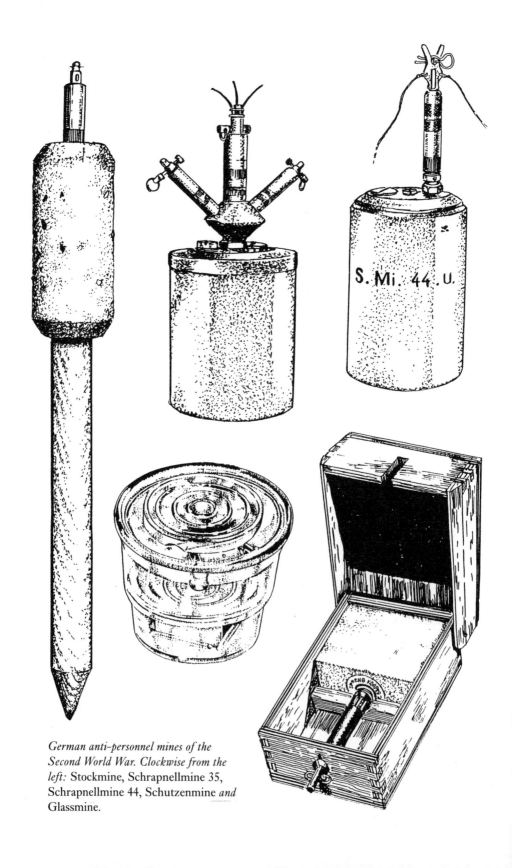

German anti-personnel mines of the Second World War. Clockwise from the left: Stockmine, Schrapnellmine 35, Schrapnellmine 44, Schutzenmine *and* Glassmine.

direct-fire weapons protected to the front by successive anti-tank and anti-personnel minefields in densities of up to 2,000 mines per km of front, with over one million laid ahead of the German attack. Tens of thousands of mines were laid during the battle by mobile detachments and Russian sources report that these claimed two thirds of all German tank casualties. Casualty figures remain contentious but Marshal Zhukov estimated that the Germans lost 42 per cent of their tanks to mines. The great depth of the defences, the interlinked fire plan, and the defenders' ferocious efforts combined to exhaust the Germans' attacking strength after sixteen days of fighting. Mines, as they had done at El Alamein, played a significant role in providing defences where no natural line existed.

Kursk marked the extent of the German advance. From then on they fought a long retreat back across the Great Plain to Berlin. Inevitably they used mines in great numbers and increasing variety to cover their withdrawal. As Rommel put it: 'If the enemy makes more than three miles progress a day, we'll build six miles depth of anti-tank screen.' The mines could be highly efficient stopping as well as slowing an advance, as another German officer related:

> At the Bobritsa bridgehead the good effect of our mines could be noted over a long period. Russian tanks that moved into the minefield, were damaged and stopped. Heavy casualties were also inflicted on strong enemy assaults which entered the minefield. Even when the terrain was favourable, the Russians did not resume their attacks either with tanks or infantry, so that our infantry enjoyed a substantial respite. This success is ascribed exclusively to mines.

The Soviets breached minefields using a combination of artillery barrage, roller tanks and metal detectors. As with all breaching operations, they took casualties, but they were more willing than others to do so. Rommel noted these profligate tendencies, claiming: 'The Russian attacks head on, with enormous expenditure of material, and tries to smash his way through by sheer weight of numbers.' There were many reports of massed waves of soldiers, or prisoners, being driven through minefields at the head of an attack.[5]

The open terrain of North Africa and Eastern Europe offered vast tracts of tankable terrain. In contrast, the broken, hillier terrain of

Italy and North-West Europe offered much more limited room for armoured manoeuvre. Tank movement was confined to roads or valleys and consequently minefields were very much smaller than in North Africa or the Eastern Front, the more varied terrain gave rise to greater varieties of mine laying. There was a much stronger emphasis on the use of anti-personnel mines as soldiers on foot had to be prevented from outflanking defended positions. And as the Germans were fighting constantly on the retreat, with little hope of advancing, they engaged in more nuisance mining to delay the Allied advance and with increasingly cunning techniques.

An American officer described some aspects of the problem in Italy:

> The scale of anti-personnel mining increased as the campaign progressed. Booby traps were planted in bunches of grapes, in fruit and olive trees, in haystacks, at road blocks, among felled trees, along hedges and walls in ravines and valleys, hillsides and terraces, along beds and banks of streams, in tyre or cart tracks along any likely avenue of approach, in possible bivouac areas, in buildings that troops might be expected to enter, and in shell or bomb craters where soldiers might be expected to take refuge. The Germans placed mines in ballast under railroad tracks, in tunnels, at fords, on bridges, on road shoulders, in pits, in repaired pot holes and in debris. Field glasses, Luger pistols, wallets and pencils were booby trapped as were chocolate bars, soap, windows, doors, furniture, toilets, demolished German equipment, even bodies of Allied and German civilians and soldiers.

Countering mines in Italy proved more difficult than in North Africa due to the more varied terrain. The British sent thirty Scorpion flail tanks to Italy, but they could not cope with the steep hill-slopes and were soon discarded. The scale of issue of mine detectors was increased from eighteen to seventy-two per US battalion but still casualties mounted. Almost a third of tank casualties were caused by mines, underscoring the significance of mines as a major anti-armour weapon.

The versatility of the landmine to change ground to the defenders' favour was demonstrated in their use to help prevent amphibious assault. During the Second World War mines were laid along the beaches of England, North Africa, the Pacific islands, Italy and the north European coasts. Amphibious landings are extremely complex demanding maritime supremacy, aerial superiority and the ability to get troops ashore faster than they can be killed. During a landing, the attackers are most vulnerable on the beaches, which are free from cover, so they present an open field of fire, and if troops can be delayed by mines, wire and other obstacles, very high casualty rates can be imposed by fire from well-prepared defences.

In the Pacific campaign, the Japanese used large hemispherical beach mines containing around 20kg of explosive detonated by pressure applied to one of two horns protruding from their sides. They were laid in up to 2m of water and were extremely potent against landing craft or vehicles. US forces on Corregidor during February 1945 found that:

> The beach was mined. Rows of 130 anti-vehicle mines were spaced seven to fifteen feet apart along one hundred and twenty-five yards of beach. All were of a kind that poked their firing mechanism out of the sand and the infantrymen skipped over them, keeping a sharp eye out for trip wires as they ran inland. But against vehicles they proved extremely effective. One of the first out, an M7 self-propelled gun hit a mine, so did an M4 Sherman tank and a jeep towing a 37mm anti-tank gun. Mines cost Colonel Postlethwaite, Commander of the 3rd Btn, 34th Infantry Regiment, 29 men and about half his vehicles.

Many Pacific islands were covered by dense vegetation with narrow tracks offering the only means of penetrating inland, which were another obvious area for planting mines. The Americans used armoured bulldozers to clear lanes through beach minefields but over 30 per cent of their tank losses during the campaign were attributed to mines.

The most extensive coastal defences of the war were the Germans' Atlantic Wall stretching from Spain to Denmark, built in response to fears of an Allied invasion of North-West Europe. Rommel was placed in charge of the defences and, following his experience in North Africa, he was clear on what was required, as he explained to his Chief Engineer, General Wilhelm Meise:

Our only possible chance will be at the beaches – that's where the enemy is always weakest. I want anti-personnel mines, anti-tank mines, anti-paratroop mines. I want mines to sink ships and mines to sink landing craft. I want some minefields designed so that our infantry can cross them, but no enemy tanks. I want mines that detonate when a wire is tripped; mines that explode when a wire is cut; mines that can be remotely controlled; and mines that blow up when a beam of light is interrupted.

To defend the Atlantic Wall the Germans were extremely thinly spread, and mobile reserves operating over such a broad area were unlikely to be able to counter-attack with sufficient speed. Rommel therefore favoured putting all efforts into stopping the invasion on the beaches and creating a narrow defensive strip inland to fight off airborne troops. He became almost obsessive about mines: 'For the first stage, that is a thousand yard strip along the coast and a similar strip along the land front, ten mines a yard will be required, making a total for the whole of France of 20 million mines. For the remainder of the zone (8,000 yards), France will require in all some 200 million mines.' In the event, by the end of May 1944 only around 5 million mines were laid, insufficient to satisfy Rommel, but enough to concern the Allies.

The first rows of obstacles were *Tellermines* fixed to slanting wooden poles placed in the surf, arranged to detonate against landing craft heading ashore. Of 517,000 foreshore obstacles, 31,000 incorporated mines. On the beaches there were anti-tank obstacles (a variety of steel and concrete tetrahedron) and rows of barbed-wire anti-personnel obstacles. Along the length of the Wall there were over 15,000 concrete fortifications; 3,000 gun batteries and minefields were laid to protect many of these and other vulnerable points. Inland there were rows of concrete dragon's teeth – concrete-block anti-tank defences, and to prevent paratroop and glider landings open areas were planted with 'Rommel's asparagus' – a series of long poles set vertically in the ground and laced with wires attached to artillery shells. Any attempt at an airborne landing would result in the wires being pulled and the shell detonating.

The Allies were well aware that the world's largest ever amphibious assault could easily grind to a halt amongst the minefields and other

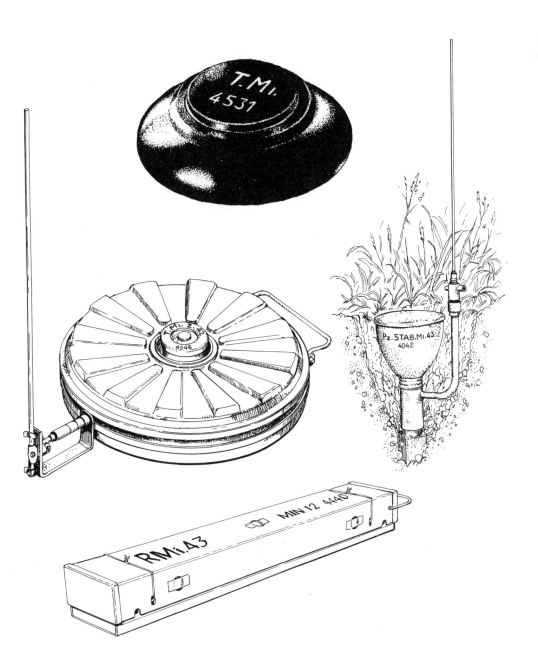

German anti-tank mines of the Second World War. Clockwise from the top: Topfmine, Panzerstabmine, Riegelmine *and* Tellermine 35 *fitted with an improvised tilt rod.*

obstacles of the Atlantic Wall. The disastrous Dieppe Raid of 1942 demonstrated how easy it was for a handful of determined defenders, tucked behind well-thought-out defences, to hold off an amphibious landing, and in particular, the difficulties of getting tanks through those defences. Tasked to overcome these problems on D-Day, Major General Percy Hobart[6] led the development of a variety of tanks innovatively designed to overcome the many obstacles they would meet during the invasion. They became known as Hobart's Funnies, and included bridgelayers, flamethrowers, trackway carriers, amphibious tanks, ramp carriers, recovery vehicles and mine-clearance tanks, including ploughs, rollers and the Sherman Crab flail. The Americans turned down the offer of Funnies to support their forces, opting instead to use detectors, bayonets and Bangalore torpedoes supported by armoured bulldozers, to breach minefields. The American refusal to use British Funnies led to a long-lasting debate, Liddell Hart claiming that 'the American troops paid dearly for the higher command's hesitation to accept Montgomery's earlier offer to give them a share of Hobart's specialised armour ... in the event they missed the Crabs the most.' Amongst the Americans there was a feeling that the British were relying too much on gadgets and not enough on brawn.

The first troops ashore on D-Day arrived in France not by sea, but from the air, by glider and parachute. There was considerable concern prior to the assault about the effects of 'Rommel's asparagus' – some commanders feared that these obstacles would account for as many as 70 per cent of landing casualties. In the event, the effect of the asparagus was overshadowed by the immense Norman hedgerows which split open many gliders on landing, accounting for 16 per cent of airborne casualties.

Twenty British landing craft at Gold Beach struck mines causing moderate to severe damage, and losing men and equipment. Underwater demolition teams had been trained and deployed to clear lanes through these obstacles, but they achieved little as German snipers concentrated their fire on them. On the beaches and in the dunes there were more mines. Men from the American 237th Engineer Combat Battalion struggled to clear a path through Utah

Beach as tanks and men behind them queued up to get through the minefields. Sergeant Vincent Powell recalled: 'Those were the first men inland and suddenly they started stepping on mines, S mines, Bouncing Betties. These mines bounced up and exploded. The men began screaming and running back to the beach with the blood just flowing.' Most of the 200 casualties on Utah Beach 'were caused by mines ... mostly those devilish S mines'. On Omaha Beach, the 115th Infantry Regiment were stalled for several hours when a rumour swept through the troops that American mine detectors could not locate German mines. The difficulties in breaching the obstacles on Omaha Beach were a key factor in the 3,000 casualties sustained there by the US forces. In contrast the British drove their Sherman Crabs off the landing craft and began flailing immediately, clearing paths up through the dunes and then back to the high-water mark. 'We were saved by our flail tanks, no question about that,' claimed Major Kenneth Ferguson.

By nightfall on D-Day, 175,000 Allied troops were established on the beachhead at a cost of around 4,900 casualties, of which perhaps 10 per cent were caused directly by mines. Mines also forced the Allies to invest considerable time and effort into devising counter-mine measures, dictating the Allies assault formation and order of battle. They did not prevent the landings but they influenced their conduct.

The practical effectiveness of mines was clear, but they also had a psychological effectiveness. Fear in soldiers was no new phenomenon – it is an entirely rational self-preservation mechanism. Mines, however, invoked a special nervousness that was articulated by US Lieutenant Teddy Bottinelli: 'The thing I hated most were the minefields ... that was the thing that put the fear of God in you. It's an eerie feeling because it is something unseen. It's there and it's not there, you know?' It was a feeling echoed by Lieutenant Colonel Sandes of the Indian Engineers, who said that many soldiers became 'so suspicious [of mines] that it is surprising that they could ever move anywhere or touch anything'. Mines, above all other weapons systems, created a fear and a paranoia that could cause delays and inhibit action in a manner that was out of

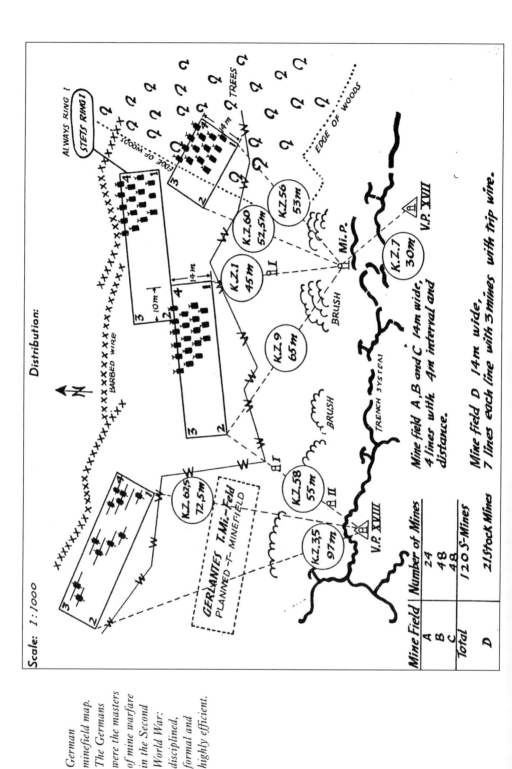

Scale: 1:1000

Distribution:

German minefield map. The Germans were the masters of mine warfare in the Second World War: disciplined, formal and highly efficient.

ALWAYS RING 1

STEFS RING 1

N

BARBED WIRE

EDGE OF WOODS

EDGE OF WOODS

TREES

4m

10m

14m

14m

K.Z.56 53m

K.Z.60 52,5m

K.Z.1 45m

K.Z.9 65m

K.Z.62,5 72,5m

GERLANTES I.Mi.—feld
PLANNED –T– MINEFIELD

K.Z.58 55m

K.Z.3,5 97m

Mi.P.

K.Z.7 30m

BRUSH

BRUSH

TRENCH SYSTEM

V.P. XVIII

V.P. XVII

Mine Field	Number of Mines
A	24
B	48
C	48
Total	120 S-Mines
D	21 Stock Mines

Mine field A, B and C 14m wide,
4 lines with 4m interval and
distance.

Mine field D 14m wide,
7 lines each line with 3 mines with trip wire.

proportion to the threat that they actually posed. This psychological impact could be extreme, as observed amongst American troops during the campaign for North-West Europe: 'Some men elected to remain erect through intensive shell fire rather than risk falling on a mine. Nothing was feared more than mines, they were insidious, treacherous things.'

The key difference from other weapons is that mines are victim operated. A soldier can quite unwittingly initiate an unseen device that will cause him terrible injuries. This can occur well away from the enemy when no threat is apparent, so the nervous strain can become quite intense. An American GI veteran of North-West Europe put it into context: 'I had gone through aerial bombing, artillery and mortar shelling, open combat, direct rifle and machine gun firing, night patrol and ambush. Against all of this we had some kind of chance; against mines we had none. The only defence was not to move.' And if a soldier initiated one, a British officer felt that there was 'something faintly derogatory about becoming a casualty from a mine; as a weapon of war it lacks the distinction of a shell or bullet. If one has to lose a foot (or one's life) it seems more respectable somehow for it to be done by a shell rather than a mine.' The psychological aspects of mine warfare were difficult to quantify yet absolutely palpable to soldiers moving through mine-infested terrain. Mines slowed down everything, forced troops to look before each step, invoked a constant gut-wrenching fear and inhibited movement.

In some ways the Second World War can be regarded as an immense war of attrition between military industrial complexes, ultimately victory being decided not by soldiers, sailors and airmen, but by economic planners, factory owners and financiers. Mines proved themselves an ideal attritional weapon: they used modest resources, were easily mass produced and cheap. They imposed on the other side the need to develop countermeasures which absorbed technical and industrial capacity, made demands on troop training times and required additional logistical capacity. An encounter with mines would inevitably impose delays on the attackers and cause casualties. Mines accounted for around 4 per cent of personnel casualties, and 20 to 30 per cent of tank losses, a similar proportion to losses caused by other tanks, so they were highly effective anti-armour weapons in their own right.

The number of mines laid was dictated by the extent of tankable terrain in any given theatre. The more tankable the terrain, the more mines were needed. But there was an inverse relationship between the number of mines laid and the proportion of casualties they caused. In North Africa and Kursk around 2,000 mines were laid per tank casualty; in the broken terrain of Italy and North-West Europe the ratio was more like 200 mines per tank casualty. The rapid increase in the number of mines laid as the war progressed was a clear indication of their importance.

Originally employed to counter tanks, mines rapidly demonstrated a utility beyond the casualties they inflicted. In the battle of materials they provided economy for the defender and imposed attrition upon the attacker. They slowed down the pace of battle and smothered attempts at blitzkrieg, with the side with armoured supremacy imposing on the other the need for more mines as the key form of defence. Methods of countering the mine were never entirely satisfactory and the initiative always remained with the defender. Of all the hazards of war the mine was the most insidious and the most feared, providing a disturbing psychological dimension. Soldiers could fight against all other weapons, but the unseen mine defied aggression. The multi-faceted effects of mines demonstrated during the Second World War ensured that they would remain an integral part of war in the future.

Notes

1   Named after Carl Gustaf Emil Mannerheim, Commander-in-Chief of Finland's
    Defence Forces, it was constructed in the early 1920s and updated in the 1930s.
2   The Finns had 5,000 M36, 85,000 M39 metal anti-tank mines, 133,000 S39 and S40
    wooden anti-tank mines and a variety of anti-personnel mines. These and other details
    can be found at the excellent website: http://www.jaegerplatoon.net/
3   Majdalany, Fred, *The Battle of El Alamein*, New York, J.B. Lippencot and Company,
    1964, p. 146.
4   After the war the Royal Engineers commissioned artist Terrence Cuneo to
    immortalize the image of the cool-headed Sapper operating a mine detector,
    concentrating intently, whilst a violent firefight rages around him. It hangs today at
    the Royal Engineers Headquarters Mess at Brompton in Kent.
5   The Allies used PoWs for mine clearance after the war and often marched lines of
    prisoners over the ground afterwards to demonstrate that it was clear. See the next
    chapter.
6   Hobart, who was born in 1885 and had served with tanks since 1920, was retired early
    in the war, in part because of his 'unconventional ideas' on armoured warfare. Basil
    Liddell Hart wrote a newspaper article criticizing the decision and shortly after,
    Hobart was reinstated by Churchill.

Chapter 6

Demining After the
Second World War

—⁓—

*The location of mines is a difficult problem ... I am afraid
that complete clearance may take a long time.*
Prime Minister Clement Atlee, October 1945

The Second World War was a period of unparalleled
destruction. Perhaps as many as 60 million people died, cities
were destroyed and economies were ruined. Post-war
governments faced a range of enormous challenges: reconstruction,
economic and social upheaval, refugee movement, mass
demobilization and food shortages, the latter brought on, in part, by
agricultural land being mined. Across Europe and North Africa there
were in excess of 100 million uncleared mines, many of which had
been buried for several years, overgrown with vegetation, sometimes
unmarked and often unrecorded. In the chaotic post-war period, with
so many competing priorities, mine clearance, or demining as it
became known, was undertaken pragmatically with over 95 per cent
of all mines laid during the war located and destroyed by 1948.

A wide variety of mine-clearance techniques were developed
during the Second World War, but these aimed to breach lanes rather
than to clear entire minefields. The difference may seem subtle, but it
soon became apparent that speed, essential for breaching, had to be
balanced against the thoroughness demanded of demining. In

combat, speed of attack was the vital factor for which attackers were prepared to trade casualties. In the post-conflict environment the equation changed. The requirement was not to breach lanes rapidly that were largely free of mines, but to clear whole minefields and return them, free of all mines, for civilian use. The wartime breaching techniques were incapable of achieving the standards required for peacetime demining. Flails and rollers were never fully effective and ploughs simply pushed mines to one side. Explosive bombardment was not a viable option in peacetime and linear charges proved capricious. The result of parallel, overlapping, mechanical or explosive breaches was an area with fewer mines but not a mine-free area as mines were pushed, thrown or displaced into previously 'cleared' lanes.

The technique of choice, adopted universally, was manual clearance using a prodder and, when available, a metal detector. It was slow, labour intensive and dangerous, but it got the job done to an acceptable standard. It was sometimes supplemented by using flamethrowers to burn off vegetation, or grappling lines to pull tripwires. But peacetime demining demanded an intimate relationship between men, mines, the ground and any vegetation that grew over the redundant minefields. It was a painstaking task, burning or cutting the vegetation, taking care not to pull any tripwires, prodding the earth every few centimetres to feel for buried mines and checking the area with a metal detector. The rate of clearance varied greatly but averaged around 100 square metres per man per day (less than half the size of a tennis court).

During the war, apart from deliberate breaching by attacking forces, armies cleared mines to make available vital ground for military use, or to retrieve mines for reuse. In the early part of the war in the North African desert, both German and Allied forces regularly cleared their own mines relatively quickly and safely as mines recently laid in sand were easy to spot and, as the Allies did not use anti-personnel mines or anti-lift devices. The Germans, who had made provision for anti-personnel devices, were able to rely on their accurate records to facilitate effective clearance. But as the war progressed, all sides made increasing use of anti-personnel devices, the thoroughness of recording declined and as a result demining became more hazardous.

Prior to 1940 there was very little experience of mine warfare in any army and demining became a new discipline which proved deceptively difficult even if there was no danger from enemy action. It demanded technique, consistency and patience – a combination that few forces possessed and attempts to clear minefields during the war inevitably resulted in high casualties. In May 1943, the US 20th Engineer Regiment was ordered to clear redundant German minefields in the Sedjenane Valley in Tunisia, ultimately clearing over 200,000 mines. It was an unpopular and costly decision as articulated by one soldier:

> Why? Virtually everyone objected. Why? The fields had no military value, they were only worked by Arabs. Removing mines was enormously difficult and dangerous, thousands of mines in thick bush and scrub that would only be trod on by Arabs and their beasts. Almost every day there were casualties ... seven officers and nineteen men killed all because someone thought it a good idea to clear the Sedjenane and nobody stopped it.

The following year in Italy, north of Naples, the US 10th Combat Engineer Battalion lost fifteen dead and forty-two injured in a sixteen-day operation to clear 20,000 mines. Few units were willing to undertake such hazardous, low-priority tasks, or could spare the time or resources in between periods of combat, so the great majority of minefields were left untouched.

After the First World War the modest numbers of mines and booby traps laid on the Western Front were cleared by the military in the immediate post-armistice period. The enormous scale of the problem after the Second World War demanded not only a military, but a broader central government response. Some of the earliest demining efforts were in parts of liberated Italy where the authorities organized demining to return land for civilian use. This was initially viewed with some suspicion by Allied forces who feared that the specialist knowledge and the explosives required for mine clearance might be used against them. But eventually the British provided instructors for five training schools that were established by the Italian Government for civilian deminers. Despite the training, casualty rates were high. One of the first demining teams, a squad of twenty-two men based in Florence, had five men seriously injured whilst clearing around 1,400 mines in a six-week period in September and October 1944, with the non-metallic *schu* mine the main cause of casualties.[1] This rate of one casualty for every 280 mines cleared was gradually improved, but 1,100 Italian deminers were killed or injured clearing around 3 million mines between 1945 and 1946.

In France, by the end of the war there were 13 million buried mines in four main areas: the Maginot Line laid in 1940, the Atlantic and the Mediterranean coasts laid in 1942–4 and across the north-west, laid during the German retreat in 1944–5. A Ministry of Reconstruction was established in November 1944 with a third of its 7.5 billion franc budget devoted to demining. Initially the French viewed demining as an opportunity to regain some national pride. Demining operations were delegated to the Ministry of Agriculture which recruited volunteers who were fit, healthy, capable of learning and imbibed with civic spirit. British Army specialists were brought in to run the first training courses at Bayeux, and detectors were provided by the British and the Americans. There are no clear statistics for pre-armistice French demining efforts, but casualties were reportedly higher than during 1945–6, when over 40 per cent of deminers were killed or injured.

The Italian and French experience was repeated in Holland where a joint military-civilian organization started demining in December 1944 in the wake of the Allied liberation. In the period to July 1945, they cleared around 85,000 mines with twenty-six killed and a further sixty-three injured.

From the initial demining efforts several aspects of the problem became clear: the task was enormous, progress would be slow and many lives would be lost. The obvious solution was to make German prisoners of war (PoWs) clear the minefields. As part of their recruit training all German soldiers received lessons in mine warfare and many of the engineer troops were mine warfare specialists, so they had the appropriate training and experience. During 1944–5, the many PoWs captured by the Allies formed a readily available source of cheap labour; although not free as working PoWs were entitled to a wage. The use of PoWs for demining was also a continuation of a much broader post-war forced-labour programme that had been agreed in principle by Stalin, Roosevelt and Churchill at the February 1945 Yalta Conference. The programme involved several million German prisoners employed on reconstruction, agricultural, mineral extraction and industrial work, in some cases until as late as 1953, across Europe, Britain and her colonies, the Soviet Union and the United States. The practical case was supported by a compelling moral argument: the Germans had started the war and laid most of the mines. Few people had any compunction about Germans becoming victims of their own mines, especially as details of wartime atrocities came to light.

The use of PoW deminers was not without controversy, with debate between the pragmatists and the humanitarian lawyers. The prevailing pragmatist stance was summarized by US Major General Baker in occupied Germany soon after the Armistice: 'We are making rather too much of the question of whether German PoWs should be employed on this work [demining]. It is inconceivable that US soldiers should now be required to undertake the removal of mines placed by the Germans. I can see no reason, legal or moral, why they should not be removed by the party that placed them.' On the other side, humanitarian lawyers pointed to Article 32 of the Third Geneva Convention of 1929, which stated: 'It is forbidden to employ prisoners of war on unhealthy or dangerous work.' Demining was not, however, expressly prohibited by the Convention which had been written after the First World War when few mines had been laid and the extent of their future use was not anticipated. But with demining operations across Europe returning casualties at an alarming rate it was clearly a dangerous activity.

The French, who were especially keen to employ PoWs for demining, sent their Foreign Minister, Georges Bidault, to press the case with the International Committee of the Red Cross (ICRC). Taking advantage of the imprecise drafting of the 1929 Convention Bidault reasoned that given the appropriate training and equipment demining was not dangerous. It was a fine argument. 'Dangerous' is a relative term and whilst training reduced the risks, it certainly did not eliminate them. The ICRC had witnessed PoW demining operations in Europe and were well aware of the steady stream of casualties sustained by them. They therefore held firm to their humanitarian principle that PoWs should not be compelled to undertake this dangerous work. Bidault stressed the Allies' moral case but recognized the strength of the ICRC's position. Ever the diplomat, he negotiated an agreement to postpone a final decision until a conference could be convened to ratify an end to PoW employment as deminers. This was eventually held in 1949, where it was confirmed that, '*Unless he be a volunteer*, no prisoner of war may be employed on labour which is of an unhealthy or dangerous nature. *The removal of mines or similar devices shall be considered as dangerous labour* [author's italics]'. In the meantime, to provide a veil of legality, PoWs attended formal training courses and were induced to volunteer for demining duties with the promise of early release, better conditions and higher rates of pay.

In many countries, there was a strong notion that the Germans should put right the damage they had inflicted and there was little sympathy for the legal humanitarian arguments or the PoWs they proposed to protect. At a symbolic ceremony at Bucheres in France, where the SS had massacred 68 civilians during the war, PoW deminers were addressed by the Préfet of L'Aube: 'The guilty party is not Hitler alone, but all his accomplices, that is to say, the whole of Germany. As for you, there is nothing more for you to do other than to cleanse your souls and repair the harm you have done.'[2] Other countries displayed a similar attitude towards German PoWs clearing minefields. In Norway the press, in an episode of undiluted *schadenfreude*, boasted about the German PoW casualties caused whilst clearing minefields: 192 killed and a further 275 wounded. In Holland, a PoW deminer, eighteen-year-old Bernhard Rath, lost a quarter of his unit whilst clearing mines along the North Sea coast. During Christmas 1945 he attended a PoW church service where a Dutch priest spoke about peace and reconciliation. On leaving the church they were attacked by local people who threw stones at them and beat them with sticks.

The Greeks, with no PoWs of their own, lobbied the British for PoW deminers. British Defence Attaché, Brigadier Kirkman, was sympathetic. It was hard for the Greeks, he argued, 'who after all did not invite the Germans to lay mines in their country', pointing out that 'the principle that German prisoners may be employed on mine clearance and exposed to serious injury or loss of life, seems to be generally accepted.' After much discussion the Greek request was refused as there was concern that PoWs would not be treated in accordance with the accepted standards and because the liability for their welfare would remain with the British. The Greeks were instead provided with 250 mine detectors to undertake the task themselves.

Tens of thousands of PoW deminers were used across Europe including France, Holland, Denmark, Norway, Britain, the Soviet Union and Germany. In France alone there were, at the peak of demining operations in November 1945, over 48,000 German PoWs (and a further 3,000 French deminers). A solid work ethic was instilled by a combination of making them feel guilty about Germany's conduct during the war and by offering early release to the hardest workers. The last were not repatriated until 1948, by which time 1,709 PoWs had been killed and a further 3,000 injured clearing around 13 million mines, a casualty rate of around 10 per cent. During the same period the French deminers lost 471 killed and 738 injured, a casualty rate of around 40 per cent. We know that these figures are underestimates as post-war record keeping was not systematic. But it is difficult to account for the much higher casualty rate amongst French civilian deminers. PoW casualties may have been significantly under reported, PoWs may have been more cautious and competent, or official statistics may have been amended to demonstrate that PoWs were engaged on less dangerous tasks than the French.

In other parts of North-West Europe, German PoWs cleared mines under the supervision of Allied troops. Over one million mines were cleared in Holland by the Draeger Brigade, under the supervision of I Canadian Corps, soon after the Armistice. The Brigade, commanded by German Engineer, Lieutenant Colonel Draeger, had over 3,300 men who were self-administered, demonstrated 'excellent control of their subunits and showed the utmost cooperation throughout'. Many of the minefields were well recorded and could be cleared in a third of the time it took to clear unrecorded minefields. If there was no minefield record, after demining an area, PoWs were 'allowed to satisfy themselves that the ground had been thoroughly searched by walking over in close order'.

The practice of marching PoWs through cleared minefields was widespread and appeared to have attracted no condemnation. There was little sympathy for the Germans and it focussed their attention on doing a thorough job. There was a degree of grandstanding in the practice, as in any demining operation cleared areas were routinely walked over. Whilst the chances of encountering a live mine in a cleared area were greatly reduced, being marched over the ground in close order, with a hostile population looking on, must have caused distinct feelings of anxiety. The practice therefore served three purposes: it encouraged thorough demining practices; it intimidated PoWs; and it gave onlookers confidence that the ground was truly safe to walk on.

The Draeger Brigade worked rapidly and kept the most detailed statistics of any demining operation. In six months they cleared 1,162,458 mines, of which 40 per cent were anti-tank mines; booby traps were fitted to 1.4 per cent of mines and on average 100 mines we lifted per sixty-two man hours. During the operation there were 290 accidents resulting in 179 men killed and a further 381 injured. *Schu* mines had a fatality rate of 2 per cent compared with 31 per cent for S mines and 60 per cent for anti-tank mines. Morale amongst PoWs fluctuated but, perhaps surprisingly, there were few desertions and discipline remained strong throughout.

In Allied occupied Germany, Labour Service Units (or *Dienstgruppen*) were organized for reconstruction and demining work. In the Aachen area a British-supervised *Dienstgruppe* of 1,340 men cleared 969 square kilometres of 760,000 mines in the two years following the end of the war, with 108 killed and 112 injured in the operation. Other PoW demining operations included the Channel islands where 300 PoWs cleared 67,000 mines, with eight killed and fourteen injured.

In countries with no PoWs, demining was largely undertaken by military engineers, with one of the largest tasks falling to the Polish. Poland was the scene of some of the heaviest fighting of the war with almost 15 million German and Soviet buried mines covering 2 per cent of the country. The range of mines was more extensive than in any other theatre of war – forty-three different types of German mine and thirty-five types of Soviet mine. The Polish Army created a force of around 10,000 deminers who cleared a remarkable 10 million mines during 1945 alone and had cleared 97 per cent of all the mines (as well as over 40 million other explosive remnants of war) by 1948. Inevitably there were casualties, with 428 killed and 593 injured between 1945 and 1948. These statistics represent around one casualty for every 15,000 mines cleared and are very much lower than the one casualty per 2,000 per mines cleared, which was a more normal figure in other theatres. This may be the result of different methods of compiling statistics or may indicate that many of the mines cleared were from stockpiles, which was intrinsically safer than clearing buried mines.

In the Soviet Union the clearance of former battlefields was viewed as a continuation of the great patriotic national effort with a combination of military, PoW and civilian volunteer groups engaged in large numbers. The Soviets claim to have cleared 58.5 million mines and a further 122 million explosive remnants of war in the post-war period. But mines continued to be found in large numbers over the following years and, even as late as 2005, 10,500 mines from the Second World War were located and destroyed. No casualty figures have been published, given the size of the task, but there may have been in the region 30,000 deminers killed and injured.

Inevitably, mines caused civilian casualties. As people started to reclaim their homes and fields they soon discovered the deadly nature of these largely unseen weapons. In France in 1945 alone, 408 people were killed and a further 556 were injured by mines. In Poland a national education programme warned the public of the danger of mines, but still around 900 people a year, with a disproportionate number of children, fell victim to mines in the early post-war years. Extrapolate these figures across the whole of Europe and the annual civilian casualty figures may well have exceeded 60,000 casualties a year in the immediate post-war era.

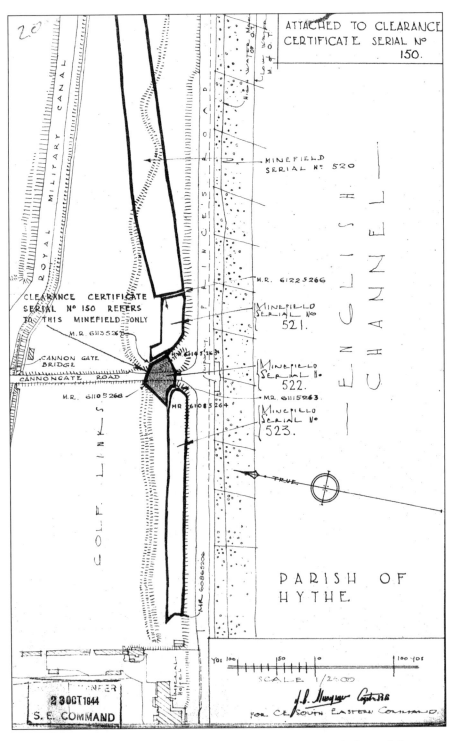

A minefield map from Hythe in Kent. Around 1,600 minefields were laid around the coast of Southern and Eastern England. They proved easier to lay than to clear.

Britain, despite not experiencing combat on land during the Second World War, also had a significant problem with mines. Fear of invasion in 1940 during the 'darkest hour' led to the hasty construction of erected defences, including trenches, pill boxes, concrete anti-tank barriers, barbed wire and beach minefields. The most commonly used mine was the B Type C which contained around 9kg of high explosive (over twice the size of a standard anti-tank mine) and was waterproofed to allow it to be laid on beaches. It was set to operate under 60kg of pressure transmitted through a top cover to an internal bow-spring which inverted to hit a striker, which in turn detonated the mine. The bow-spring proved to be a critical design flaw. As the mines aged and corroded, it weakened dramatically, thereby reducing the operating pressure and making it liable to detonate on the slightest pressure.

In 1940, 350,000 mines were laid in 1,600 minefields, on beaches that might be used by German invaders, along much of southern and eastern England. In 1940, few soldiers had received any mine training and in the chaotic months following the Dunkirk evacuation minefields were laid in a very haphazard manner, with minimal recording. It was appreciated that clearing the mines would not be easy, but the extent of the difficulties had not been fully grasped and the repercussions lasted for decades.

By 1943, after the 'turning of the tide', when the threat of German invasion had receded, the minefields were redundant and many beaches were needed to train troops for the D-Day landings. Furthermore the public demanded clearance to allow access to the sea and to prevent civilian casualties. The Director of Local Defence in Southern England complained in December 1942 that 'fatalities due to beach mines have already been very serious, somewhere in the region of 200 casualties.'

Demining was essentially a new discipline in 1943, so tools and techniques were largely experimental. There were few accurate minefield records, so often it was unclear which areas were mined and how many mines had been laid and thus how many mines needed to be retrieved. Added to these general difficulties were the particular problems of mined beaches. Wave and tidal forces exposed some

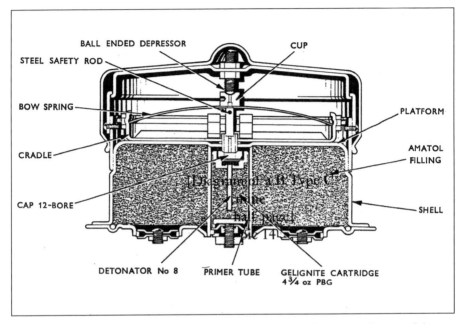

STEEL SAFETY ROD
BALL ENDED DEPRESSOR
CUP
BOW SPRING
PLATFORM
CRADLE
AMATOL FILLING
CAP 12-BORE
SHELL
DETONATOR No 8
PRIMER TUBE
GELIGNITE CARTRIDGE 4¾ oz PBG

A British B Type C mine. 350,000 were laid on the beaches of Britain at the start of the Second World War. The last were recovered in the 1990s.

mines, but caused others to be deeply buried under sand or shingle, or to migrate outside marked minefields. The problems were compounded by the increasing sensitivity of the B Type C mine. During heavy weather, mines tossed around in the surf would often detonate. They could also be set off by animals – a dog strayed into a minefield in Kimmerage Bay in Dorset and set off a mine which, as a result of sympathetic detonation, initiated eighty mines on the beach. At Selsey Bill in Hampshire, a group of holidaymakers were surprised (although none were injured) when they detonated a mine when throwing stones on the beach.

The B Type C mine had one redeeming characteristic: it contained over 10kg of metal and could be detected by the Polish mine detector at ranges of over 60cm. But against this, many mines were buried under more than 60cm of sand and the Polish mine detector, always in short supply throughout the war, was unreliable in wet conditions. A larger detector, known as the ERA (Electronic Research Agency) locator, was developed during the war. It required two men to operate it and could detect B Type C mines at a range of 150cm. But it was fragile and was sensitive to the smallest fragments of metal, so it was of uncertain reliability and produced a high number of alarms, all of which had to be investigated.

The clearance technique eventually adopted involved the use of a high-pressure water jet mounted on a tracked Bren gun carrier to expose buried mines. In areas of heavy deposition, layers of gravel and sand were stripped aside by armoured bulldozers before using the water jet. The area was then swept with metal detectors. It proved an imprecise science and this was reflected in different types of clearance certificates issued, as follows:

1. All mines have been accounted for.

2. Not all mines have been accounted for but the area has been swept by detector. Though no guarantees can be given, the area can be considered safe except for the possibility of mines being washed up from other fields.

3. The area has been disturbed by sea, wind, cliff falls or enemy action. The area has been swept but there remains a remote possibility of mines being found.

During the war clearance of the beaches was undertaken by the Royal Engineers, with assistance from the Canadians and others. During this time 118 men were killed and a further thirty-five injured. The high fatality rate reflects the very large explosive charge in the B Type C mine – anyone within 5m of the mine when it detonated was invariably killed. Priority for clearance was given to areas needed for the war effort. Lower priority and technically challenging areas, such as those with deeply buried mines, were left until after the war, and in July 1945 there remained over 60,000 mines in 375 mined areas around the coast. Prime Minister Atlee explained the problem to the House of Commons in October 1945: 'The location of mines is a difficult problem, particularly as many have been shifted by tides and soil movements ... I am afraid that complete clearance may take a long time.' The Royal Engineers aimed to clear all minefields by the summer of 1947, but this proved greatly optimistic.

Whilst pressure to clear the remaining minefields mounted, the manpower available to carry out the task was being demobilized. The obvious solution, working elsewhere in Europe, was to employ German PoWs. By the end of the war there were around 200,000 German and 150,000 Italian PoWs in the UK. Many were employed on agricultural work and were highly regarded for their work ethic and discipline.[3] Following the French example, the War Office agreed in October 1945 that German PoWs could be used for mine clearance, 'provided that they were adequately trained and normal safety precautions were taken'.[4] It proved a surprisingly long and mutually satisfying relationship with official reports claiming that the PoWs 'completely integrated into the close-knit team' of Royal Engineers Bomb Disposal units. In 1946, around 1,200 PoWs were employed on demining duties in Britain. In 1948, they were eligible for repatriation but many from Ukraine, who had fought for the Germans, chose to remain in the UK as civilian employees of the Royal Engineers rather than return to an uncertain fate in their Soviet-occupied homeland. In 1952, their additional pay for dangerous work was withdrawn (only three were killed between 1946 and 1952) and 189 of the remaining 330 Ukrainian deminers left for better paid work. But the remaining 141 formed an integral and highly valued part of the Royal Engineers Bomb Disposal family for many years. The last former PoW, Steve Marynuik, retired in 1990. To honour the Ukrainians' contribution the officers of the Royal Engineers Bomb Disposal Regiment purchased for their Mess a silver statue of Saint Volodymyr – the patron Saint of Ukraine.

In contrast to the long and fulfilling relationship between Britain and the Ukrainian PoWs, the relationship between Britain and beach mines proved long and frustrating. Between July 1945 and December 1948, 61,000 mines in 369 minefields had been cleared at a cost of thirty-three killed and nineteen injured. In recognition of the dangers of the task, the General Service Medal (GSM) was issued to those involved at the sharp end of bomb and mine clearance duties for 180 days or more. It was the first such medal to be awarded for service in the United Kingdom. In 1949, there remained over a thousand mines in seven minefields, mostly in East Anglia and in areas where cliff falls had made clearance especially difficult. It was 1972 before the last remaining beach minefield at Trimmingham, Norfolk, was opened to the public, and only then after much hand wringing. The great North Sea storm of 1953 had exposed 350 mines along the East coast. Southwold beach, also on the East coast, had been demined after the war but by 1958 a further twelve mines had been found. The concern was such that the area was again searched and two more mines were located. In 1960 a new seawall was built and contractors unearthed five mines submitting a claim to the MoD for £11,842 to compensate for the delays incurred (the MoD eventually paid £6,797). Despite the intensive demining efforts, dozens of mines were found along the coast each year. The last B Type C mines, a group of eight, were cleared from Whitsand Bay in Cornwall in 1998 – forty-eight years after they were laid.

Numbers of mines cleared from the British beaches by decade				
1950s	1960s	1970s	1980s	1990s
1,360	530	376	397	23

The GSM was also awarded for work on pipe mines that were laid under airfields across the country. These were command-initiated demolition charges; each pipe was over 5 metres long and they were laid in great lattices under the hundreds of airfields that were constructed around the country at the start of the war. Had Britain been invaded the pipe mines would have been detonated to destroy the airfields to prevent the Germans from using them. Most of the pipe mines were removed at the end of the war in parallel with the beach minefield clearance, but some remained and dozens have been removed since the end of the war by the Royal Engineers, as part of Operation Crabstick, the most recent in 2006 at Lee-on-Solent in Hampshire.[5]

The pipe mines caused few casualties, unlike the beach mines. We know that 155 deminers lost their lives clearing the beaches, but it is much more difficult to establish the civilian cost as no figures were compiled. In 1942, one estimate was of 200 fatalities. In one of the worst accidents, five boys aged between eleven and thirteen were killed by a beach mine at Swanage, Dorset in 1955, in an area that had been demined several times. And there were many other reported mine casualties around the coast, at least into the 1950s. So in all perhaps 500 people, military and civilian, were killed by the British beach minefields. How effective they might have been in the event of an invasion is, as always, difficult to disaggregate from the overall defensive effort. They certainly would have caused the Germans to spend effort devising and deploying countermeasures, and they would have inflicted casualties.

The costs, financial and especially human, of the post-war demining operations across Europe were enormous. Certainly tens of thousands, and possibly hundreds of thousands of people, deminers and civilians, were killed and injured by redundant mines. This represents a small proportion of the 60 million or so that died during the war, but it remains a significant number. The stoical attitudes of the times and the broad range of challenges facing the post-war world relegated the significance of the casualties. It was an era before health and safety regulations when the price of life, especially a PoW's life, was cheap. The achievements of the post-war deminers were in many ways remarkable. The vast majority of mines, perhaps 100 million, were cleared within three years of the end of the war although, inevitably, small numbers of mines continued to be discovered decades after they were laid. The double-edged nature of mines had become apparent. They were undoubtedly effective as a defensive weapon, but they also inflicted a considerable toll long after they had become redundant. Perhaps the most surprising aspect was that the post-war demining experience did not result in the development of more efficient equipment or procedures. In contrast, considerable investment was poured into the development of new generations of mines incorporating the latest technology.

Notes

1 WO204/2482, Training of Italian Civilians for Mine Clearance, December 1944. Mine-clearance schools were established in Capua, Viterbo, Chieti, Spoleto and Pisa.
2 Danielle Voldman's 1985 book *Attention Mines 1944-47* (written in French) is a useful account for demining in France.
3 My grandfather befriended a German PoW through the church in Hull. For many years after he was repatriated the PoW sent my grandfather food parcels and my grandfather made his first and only trip overseas to Germany to visit him in the 1950s.
4 They were provided with two months of training and with three men killed and one injured, their accident rate was far lower than their British counterparts.
5 For years the RAF have been forced to endure this joke. RAF personnel are known to the British Army as 'Crabs'. Crabstick was an inspired choice for such an operation.

Chapter 7

Preparing for the Third World War

—꽁—

*Mines are amongst the best artificial obstacles – they are portable,
installed relatively easily and constitute a hazard to the enemy.*
US Army Field Manual, 1966

The Soviet Union ended the Second World War with an army
of over 11 million men – the most powerful ever assembled.
After 1945, much of the army was demobilized, with infantry
units reduced by two thirds, but such was the confidence in tank units
that their strength was maintained. Relations between the Soviet
Union and the West deteriorated into the Cold War with the West
fearing a Soviet invasion. Countering the threat of overwhelming
armoured forces swarming across the Great European Plain was one
of the greatest challenges for NATO (North Atlantic Treaty
Organisation) military planners for nearly half a century.

To stop armoured attacks, static fortifications such as the Maginot
Line had little credibility and the doctrine called for a more flexible
defence. Artillery was highly effective against infantry in the open,
but made little impact on closed-down armoured formations. Aircraft
had been used for area bombing in the Second World War, but they
were ineffective against moving tanks until the introduction of
ground-attack aircraft in the 1970s (US A1 Huey Cobra attack
helicopter, and the A10 Thunderbolt jet). To stop armoured forces

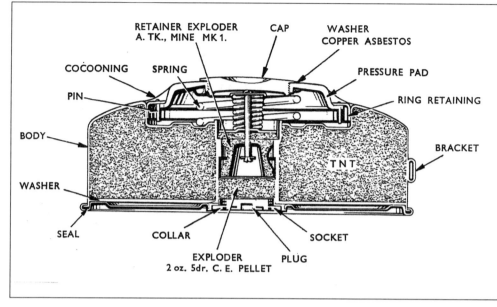

Cross section of a British Mark 7 anti-tank mine.

(in other words blitzkrieg) there were three options: first, short-range anti-tank guns, missiles and rockets operated by the infantry with a range of several hundred metres; second, other tanks which carried a larger gun, with a range of up to 2 kilometres, and combining this firepower with armoured protection and good mobility; finally, there were mines which could damage tanks and create an area in which anti-tank guns and defending tanks could be used much more effectively. NATO planned for an integrated defence using all options, including a massive minefield along the inner German border from the coast in the north to Czechoslovakia in the south.

NATO sought to ensure that this minefield was as effective as possible, which led to a constant cycle of development of new mines. We often think of the arms race being about nuclear weapons, but there was also a strong imperative to develop other ever more sophisticated weapons including mines. In broad terms, during the course of the Cold War there were three generations of mines: first, simple pressure mines; then mines that attacked the full width of a tank and had self-neutralization features; and finally, scatterable mines delivered by aircraft or artillery complete with sophisticated attack and self-neutralization features. Mine designers had to consider a variety of factors. How to stop a tank, either by immobilizing it by breaking its tracks, or 'killing' it by causing massive damage to the machine and its crew. These effects needed to be predictable and consistent so mines needed to be reliable even when buried in the wet soil of northern Europe. Counter-counter-measures had to be built into mines so that they could not easily be detected or overcome. Size and weight were important factors. Mines had to carry a charge of sufficient size to damage a tank, but the bigger the mine the greater the logistics effort required. It was also important, especially in a fast-moving, mobile battle, to lay mines rapidly using as few men as possible. And cost became an important factor as mines became more sophisticated and expensive. In the search for the perfect mine, during the Cold War, over 500 designs were brought into service worldwide.

The UK introduced several new mines at the start of the Cold War. A conventional, round, anti-tank mine, known as the Mark 7, was introduced in 1950. With nearly 9kg of TNT it had one of the heaviest main charges of any mine and was designed to break the tracks of the largest tanks with only half of the mine covered by a tank track. It had an option of three fuses: a simple pressure-operated fuse; a double-impulse pressure fuse which was designed to defeat rollers by detonating the mine, not on the first pressure received, but on the second; and a tilt-rod fuse which incorporated a 0.7-second delay to ensure that a tank would be fully over the mine before it detonated. It was an effective mine but it was slow to lay and its heavy weight made demands on the logistics chain, especially as its round shape made for inefficient packaging.

To protect the Mark 7 from manual breaching teams there were several anti-personnel mines available. First was the Mark 2 bounding fragmentation mine which had been introduced in the early 1940s. Whilst bounding fragmentation mines were used successfully by other armies, the British never really took to them and by the 1960s it had become obsolete.[1] Other anti-personnel mines were the No. 6 and No. 7. The No. 6, introduced in 1948, was 19cm long and 4cm in diameter, topped by a three-pronged pressure piece. It is easy to see how it got its nickname, the 'Carrot Mine'. It was plastic cased, with a removable metal detector ring and was designed to be difficult to detect not only using electronic detectors but also by prodding. Its slender diameter meant that a breaching lane one metre across needed to be prodded fifty times to ensure the mine was located. But it proved unreliable in wet conditions and its length made it difficult to lay on hard ground.

The other new anti-personnel mine was the No. 7 which was known, for reasons that remain unclear, as the 'Dingbat'. This was a small round mine, 6cm in diameter and 3 cm deep, made of pressed steel containing a charge of only 50 grams and capable of functioning either way up. Uniquely, it was issued with its own camouflage jacket, a piece of green and brown towelling glued to the casing. It was the first mine that was designed to be scattered by hand and implicit in this function was the proposition that surface-laid mines could still be effective. Enemy forces could breach a scatterable, surface-laid minefield more rapidly than a buried one, but the time saved in laying it was adequate compensation. This was to become a significant equation and it opened the way for the development of highly sophisticated scatterable mine systems.

The combination of Mark 7 anti-tank mines with its variety of fuses, interlaced with two or three types of anti-personnel mine, if laid in sufficient depth and numbers, was a formidable obstacle, especially if blended with natural defences, covered by fire and backed up by an armoured mobile reserve. It was not unique to the British and similar systems were used by all military forces in the early part of the Cold War. The Americans used combinations of large, round, anti-tank mines (the M6) and tripwire-operated, anti-personnel mines (M2, M3, M16), more normally called 'Bouncing Betties'. The Soviet Union continued to use wooden anti-tank mines, but also introduced the round metal TM46. For anti-personnel mines they relied on a cast-iron version of the German concrete *stockmine*, known as the POMZ, and on a copy of the German wooden *schu* mine known as the PMD 6 (both POMZ and PMD6 became some of the most widely copied and deployed mines). Although these mines were new, they essentially represented an assimilation of German mine warfare technology and methods. The Korean War of 1950–1954 provided an operational test for some of the new mines and created a demand for the development of more sophisticated types.

In previous wars tankable terrain dictated the style of mine warfare and Korea was no exception. The country was dominated by hills and mountains separated by deep, narrow valleys, there was extensive forest cover and an underdeveloped road network. With such limited tankable ground it was never going to be a war of massed armoured confrontations. Indeed, at the start of the war the South Koreans had no tanks and no anti-tank mines to stop the North's invasion. They relied largely on short-range, hand-held, anti-tank weapons and only managed to avoid being completely overrun, having yielded 90 per cent of their territory, by the narrowest of margins. UN forces (predominantly US) arrived to prevent the fall of South Korea and for the next four years fighting ebbed and flowed across the Korean peninsula. The restricted terrain resulted in few open tank battles so mines were responsible for a higher proportion of tank casualties – over 50 per cent of the total. Another indication of the restricted tank mobility was that only around eighty mines were deployed for each tank casualty, compared with 2,000 mines laid per tank casualty in the much flatter countryside of North-West Europe in 1944–5.

In the confines of Korea's narrow valleys, mines often had to be laid on sealed roads which made them easy to spot. They could be covered with earth or debris, but this still alerted tank crews to the presence of mines and they could be pushed aside using dozer blades. To achieve surprise, US Military Advisor, Major R.I. Crawford, described how two South Korean engineers 'each ran twice across the road dropping M6 mines in the path of tanks' resulting in all four tanks being knocked out. This set of circumstances caused the US to review how they might attack tanks from the side, without having to lay mines on sealed roads, and for soldiers to avoid the extreme risk of running out in front of advancing tanks. The answer was the 'off-route' mine, a mine that attacked the side of the tank – a concept that had been improvised by the Germans on the Eastern Front. The US version was based on a bazooka anti-tank rocket,[2] concealed on the side of a road up to 30m from a target and initiated by a tank as it crossed an activation wire. It was known as the M24 but was not issued for service until after the Korean War. Off-route mines were subsequently incorporated into the inventories of most modern armies where they fulfil a particular niche in mine warfare.[3]

What the Korean War lacked in armoured action, it compensated in infantry action. The Chinese proved exceptionally brave and skilled light infantry fighters, often creeping up on positions at night and launching wave after wave of attack, sustaining very high casualty rates in the process. In response, UN forces used anti-personnel mines in considerable quantities and often to good effect. At Yodoktong, US Major David Campbell described how 'almost an entire company [of Chinese] got inside the first belt of mines before they hit the first tripwire and realized their predicament. Mines exploded and men screamed. The attackers turned in panic only to kick up more tripwires. The whole affair lasted less than five minutes yet we estimated a hundred casualties.' Major Campbell also observed that when defending Sinnyong, 'the shrewd use of mines allowed the Division to straighten its line and shift a maximum number of men to the offensive,' once again demonstrating that the effective use of mines provided economies for the defender whilst imposing attrition upon the attacker.

Chinese massed infantry attacks prompted the search for a weapon with a highly destructive capability. Machine guns were effective, especially when they had open fields of fire such as those common between the trenches in the First World War. In the hills and forests of Korea, machine guns were rarely able to use their range as attackers could get close to positions before charging. Airburst shrapnel artillery shells could not be used very close to defenders' positions and did not always have the immediacy or the accuracy required. The answer was the M18A1 directional fragmentation mine, better known as the 'Claymore'. The Claymore traces its lineage from the fougasse and was designed to stop massed attacks by explosively projecting an arc of steel balls. The mine consists of a convex plastic case, 22cm long and 12cm wide, supported on a pair of scissor-like legs which allow it to be pushed into the ground and

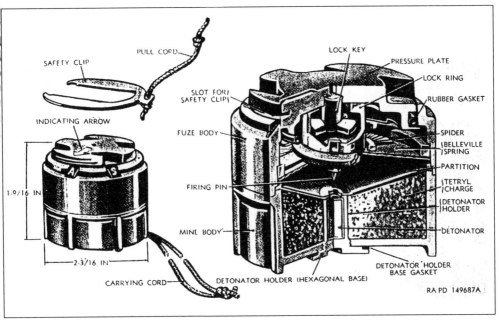

The US M14 'Toe Popper' anti-personnel mine produced after the Korean War.

aimed. It contains 680 grams of explosive and 700 steel balls. On detonation the steel balls are projected in a 60° arc calculated to have a 10 per cent chance of hitting a man at 100m, increasing to a 100 per cent chance at 50m. The mine was designed specifically to ensure that the fragments had a velocity of 1,200 metres per second, sufficient to cause a lethal injury. The Claymore was supplied with the option of command detonation, victim operation (tripwire) or time delay. It was issued too late for service in Korea, but it spawned a wide range of imitations that have been used in most conflicts ever since.

Another significant feature of mine warfare in Korea was poor recording and marking which resulted in many troops becoming casualties of their own mines. Lieutenant Sam D. Starobin, S2, 65th Engineer Combat Battalion recalled:

Mines are double-edged weapons. Properly employed they can be a strong instrument of defense. Improperly used they are a menace … A large percentage of the mines that destroyed our vehicles and killed our troops had been relaid by the enemy. American mine warfare doctrine is sound, but after the Eighth Army had shipped 120,000 mines to units, only 20,000 were recorded or on hand. The remaining 100,000 were either abandoned or buried unrecorded!

In one incident Australian forces suffered fifty casualties when they unwittingly entered a UN minefield.

As Starobin noted, the Chinese often demonstrated an ability to clear tripwire-operated mines in advance of an attack or to reuse against UN forces, thereby exposing a weak link in the US arsenal. All the US anti-personnel mines in Korea were tripwire-operated fragmentation mines, but they had no pressure-operated anti-personnel mines that could be buried to protect them. This was a surprising omission given the difficulties that the schu mine had caused US troops in the Second World War. The gap in capability was filled by the M14 pressure-operated, anti-personnel mine which contained only 29 grams of explosive in a plastic casing measuring less than 6cm in diameter by 4cm high. Its small size earned it the nick name 'Toe popper'. Like the off-route mine and the Claymore, it was produced too late for service during the war, but around 1.5 million were retained for use in Korea afterwards.

Shortcomings in the marking and recording of mines were recognized in Korea and in every theatre where mines were used. German mine-recording methods had become more or less standard amongst most armies after 1945, but their application lacked consistency and discipline even in professional armies. At a fundamental level, passing information whilst engaging with the enemy is very difficult, doubly so if changes of units or location are involved. Performance could be improved by training, but mine-warfare training was rarely provided evenly or thoroughly. In training, infantry and armour units had a habit of disregarding minefields, or at best paying lip service to them. Field Marshal Nigel Bagnell[4] noted that 'given some live mines ... dash would be replaced by caution, determination by prudence and contempt by healthy respect'. Of all military disciplines, mine warfare is one of the most difficult to teach. Engineers enjoy construction and demolition,[5] but putting mines in the ground, surrounding them by wire and recording the details is dull and unpleasant. Infantry and armour enjoy maneuvring around the field and firing their weapons, but accounting for the presence of mines inhibits their freedom of action. So soldiers have a natural propensity to avoid realistic mine-warfare training and they pay the penalty in war.

Mine clearance capabilities in Korea were little more advanced than they had been in the Second World War. The North used predominately wooden mines – copies of the German *Holz* (anti-tank) and *schu* (anti-personnel) mines which made electronic detectors of little value. The mountainous terrain made mechanical clearance less effective, so on unsealed roads the entire top surface was sometimes excavated using an entrenching tool pulled from side to side to prevent pressure being applied to the top of any mine. The principle means of detection was the keen eye and the sharp bayonet. Dan Rashen, a Royal Engineers officer, remarked on discovering two PMD6 anti-personnel mines with a prodder: 'The exceptional thing about [them] ... was that we had actually found them without harm being done. I never heard of any others being found except by claiming a target.'

Mines were responsible for around 4 per cent of US Army personnel casualties in Korea. No figures exist for North Korean and Chinese casualties but given their predilection for massed attacks through minefields, it is safe to assume they were very much higher. US and Korean planners believed that if mines had been used to defend against the North Korean invasion they would have had a much better chances of repelling, or at least slowing down, the advance. As a result of this assessment, the extensive use of mines was incorporated into South Korea's defensive plan with important implications for the International Campaign to Ban Landmines some forty years later.

That the Korean War was a close-run thing was demonstrated by President Truman's hint that nuclear weapons might be used to avert military defeat. The episode remains controversial, but he probably had in mind the delivery by aircraft of a device in a similar fashion to those dropped with such devastating effect on Hiroshima and Nagasaki. The British were also developing a nuclear capability in the

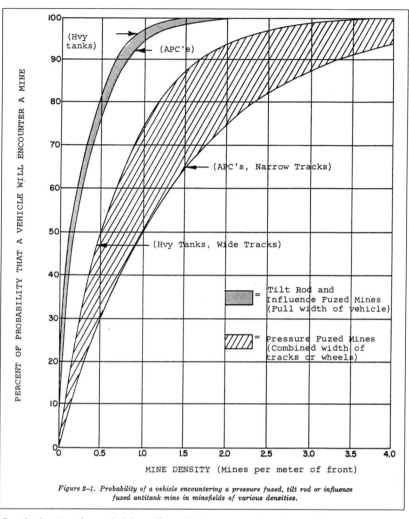

Figure 2–1. Probability of a vehicle encountering a pressure fuzed, tilt rod or influence fuzed antitank mine in minefields of various densities.

Graph showing the probability of a vehicle encountering mines. There was an ever-increasing demand to make mines and minefields more efficient.

1950s with the introduction of free-fall nuclear bombs delivered by the V range bombers, all of which is public knowledge. However, the plans for nuclear mines in the British arsenal have only recently come to light. Code-named Blue Peacock, the British nuclear mine was a 10-kiloton[6] device weighing 5.5 tons, and was designed to destroy airfields, docks, tunnel complexes and industrial areas in Europe in the event of a Soviet invasion. Strictly speaking this was a demolition charge rather than a mine, but it was termed a mine and it was to be operated by Royal Engineers who requested that five devices be provided by 1959. The mine was designed to be emplaced underground and fired by a timer after up to a week, or by anti-handling devices. There was concern that if the electronics got cold they would render the mine unserviceable, so careful consideration was given to providing insulation. Options included sealing live chickens around the casing with supplies of food and water – their body heat would apparently have been sufficient to prevent the electronics freezing.[7] Had the mine detonated underground it would have produced a crater 200m in diameter and the safety distance for friendly troops was a minimum of 30km.[8] Amidst fears about the radioactive fall-out and the viability of the initiation mechanism, the plans were shelved in 1958.

The Korean War had once again underlined the importance of mines which, as the Royal Engineers Planning Staff concluded in 1960, were 'the only practical means by which natural obstacles can be made more effective or which can be used to create an artificial barrier'. The focus changed from the effectiveness of individual mines to the broader efficiency of whole minefields. Even though it had only been in service for ten years, the Mark 7 minefield was viewed as expensive, slow and logistically cumbersome. The search for greater efficiency caused a closer examination of the long, narrow mines that had been used by the Italians and Germans during the Second World War. The result was the Barmine, 120cm long and 11cm wide; it was made of plastic, but had a removable detector plate and could be fitted with single- and double-impulse fuses.[9]

A long mine had a far greater chance of being hit by a tank than a round mine, so fewer were needed. Its square profile made it easy to pack, requiring only one eighth of the logistics effort of the Mark 7, while its shape lent itself well to mechanical laying. Machines had been developed to bury round mines but they were never very reliable. By contrast, the Barmine layer was a model of simplicity, opening a furrow in the ground and delivering mines into it using a simple conveyor with no electrical or hydraulic parts. A minefield with Barmines could be laid four times faster than a minefield with Mark 7s, with one third of the manpower. So the Barmine represented considerable advantages over its older, rounder cousin, and entered service with the British Army in 1969.

Type of Mine	No. Required	Cost £	Time to Lay	3-ton Loads
Mark 7	1,800	18,000	6.5 hours	8
Barmine	900	13,500	1.5 hours	1.25

In the early 1960s the British Army replaced its stock of unreliable No. 6 'Carrot mines' with the C3A1 Canadian anti-personnel mine, better known as the 'Elsie'. This was half the height of the No. 6, but still distinctly carrot-shaped. It too was plastic, although it had a removable detector ring. Unusually for an anti-personnel mine it contained a small shaped charge designed to pierce boot and foot. However, the real innovation in British anti-personnel mines was the upgrading of the No. 7 Dingbat into a mine that could be scattered on the ground, quickly and in large numbers. Known as 'Ranger', it was a small plastic mine fired from a discharger with seventy-two barrels, each containing eighteen mines (a total of 1,296 mines). The discharger was mounted on a truck or an armoured vehicle and had a range of around 100 metres. Ranger was designed to be fired over an anti-tank minefield or to create instant minefields. It entered service in the mid 1970s and together with the Barmine it briefly provided Britain with one of the best barrier minefield concepts of any army, although little thought had been given to how they might recover the mines after use.[10]

The US programme of mine development was to make the British efforts appear somewhat modest. In the 1950s they had established Operation Doan Brook, a feasibility study of air-delivered mines. Air-delivered mines did not just speed up the process of laying mines, they provided a capability to create minefields many miles inside enemy territory, inhibiting movement, causing casualties, and disrupting supply lines and assembly areas for attacks. Here was a way of diminishing the intensity of any Soviet attack before it even reached the first barrier minefield. A US copy of the German SD2 Butterfly Bomb, known as the M83, was used in Korea and such was the potential of the system that by the 1960s three types of air-delivered mines were available: the Wide Area Anti-Personnel Mine (WAAPM), the Dragon's tooth mine and the Gravel mine.

The WAAPMs were small steel spheres containing an explosive charge initiated by tripwires that discharged from the mine after it hit the ground. A single dispenser slung under an aircraft held 540 mines. It came in two variants: the BLU 42 which fragmented on detonation and the BLU 54 which bounded a metre in the air before detonating. Both versions were designed to self-sterilize after thirty days. The Dragon's Tooth[11] (BLU43/44) was a small, scatterable, anti-personnel, blast mine shaped roughly like a W, with one wing containing a 9-gram explosive charge, the centre containing the fuse and the other wing flattened to slow its descent. It had a self-sterilization facility and was dispensed in a bombing unit, containing 4,800 mines. The Gravel mine, which came in a number of variants,[12] was a canvas pouch containing a sensitive explosive charge that could be detonated by pressure alone. The larger Gravel mines contained a chemical designed to self-sterilize, and were dispensed from units containing between 1,500 and 7,500 mines. More than 37 million Gravel mines were produced between 1967 and 1968.

The location of air-delivered scatterable mines could not be marked, indeed when dropped, at great speed and in enormous numbers, their location was often unclear. Faith was placed in the self-sterilization mechanisms, which, even if 99 per cent reliable, still left large numbers of unmarked, unrecorded mines in areas likely to be traversed by soldiers and civilians alike. In addition to air-dropped mines, the US developed a variety of cluster munitions in the 1960s that were used in Vietnam, and it was often difficult to distinguish between the two. Cluster munitions were designed to overcome the difficulties of hitting a target, with large free-fall bombs, from a moving aircraft. Many small bombs (cluster munitions) had a far better chance of striking the target than one large one. Cluster munitions often combined two effects in a single bomblet: the first, if they hit a hard target such as a fortified position or an armoured vehicle, was a shaped charge that could pierce concrete or steel; the second was a shrapnel effect to destroy soft targets, such as human flesh. A cluster of, say 500 bombs, released from an aircraft, was designed to strike the ground in an oval pattern 300m long and 100m wide. Inevitably a percentage would not function as designed. These failed cluster munitions then assumed the characteristics of air-dropped mines, liable to detonate if moved, but without any self-neutralizing mechanism.

By the 1970s, many countries had developed a closer interest in mine warfare. The Israeli-Arab wars of 1956, 1967 and 1973 provided a microcosm of how a NATO-Soviet clash in Europe might be fought, as the Israelis used US weapons against Arab armies supplied by the Soviets. The wars appeared to demonstrate the importance of mines as an anti-armour weapon. At around this time, smaller, more sophisticated and reliable electronics became available. These made possible a new generation of mines with magnetic-influence fuses that sensed the magnetic field of a tank, firing the mine when it judged the tank to be directly overhead which, combined with a shaped charge,[13] made for a highly destructive mine. They came complete with self-neutralizing options to mitigate against the difficulty of clearing redundant minefields. One of the earliest mines of this generation, in service by 1982, was the Swedish FFV 028 which had a pre-set self-neutralization period of between thirty and 180 days, and was resistant to a range of countermeasures. In the late 1970s, they cost around $600 each, compared with the Barmine at around $20. The FFV 028's price did not deter the German, Dutch or Canadian armed forces buying them, or France, Finland and the US from developing similar mines of their own. This also provides a snapshot of the dilemma of defence spending. After only ten years the Barmine was superseded by the new generation of high-tech mines and replacing them would cost thirty times as much as the original. A compromise was found in the form of a bolt-on magnetic-influence fuse which made possible attacks across the full width of a tank, but without the devastating force of a shaped charge.

In the 1970s, there was a move towards plastic anti-personnel mines. In part this was to counter the ease with which anti-tank mines with high metal contents (electronic packages and copper-lined shaped charges) could be located with a metal detector. But it was also a reflection that the newly available range of plastics were ideal materials from which to make mines. Plastic was cheap, moulded to any form, waterproof and corrosion resistant. Even if it could be located with a metal detector, there would be a strong rationale for using it in mines. Plastic mines from this era include the German DM-11, Belgian NR409, Spanish P4A and Chinese Type 72, and are more correctly termed minimum metal mines. Typically these mines have plastic casings, but contain small metal parts such as firing pins, detonators and springs. This is an important point as it means that they can normally be located, albeit with varying degrees of difficulty, using a sensitive metal detector. And unlike the new generation of high-tech anti-tank mines, they were very cheap, and easy to use.

The Israeli-Arab wars had demonstrated that modern war was fast, highly mobile and that, even with excellent intelligence, surprise attacks were possible. Highly destructive, full-width attack mines and plastic mines were very effective, but the question was: could they be emplaced in time to stop a rapid attack? A new range of scatterable mine systems were seen as the answer. Short-range scatterable anti-personnel mines had been around for some years – the challenge now was to develop long-range scatterable anti-tank mines that were robust enough to survive the impact of landing after being dispensed from ground vehicle, helicopters, fast jet or artillery piece. By the end of the 1980s all four options were available following a period that saw considerable investment in mine warfare.

Scatterable mine systems were developed by the French, Germans and Italians. The German Skorpion system, for example, had a series of launching tubes mounted on a highly mobile tracked vehicle, and could lay 600 mines in a field 1,500 long and 100 metres wide in about five minutes using a crew of two. It used an AT2 mine with a full-width attack capability, a shaped charge and a self-neutralization mechanism. Delivered in 1986, it made the fifteen-year-old Barmine look a long way out of date in terms of effectiveness and efficiency.

Some of the earliest and most effective helicopter-delivered mines were developed by Italian companies. The Italians had been mine innovators in the early part of the Second World War, but had little involvement until the 1970s when Valsella,[14] and two other companies founded by former Valsella employees, Technovar and Misar, won contracts to supply mines to the Italian Army. In 1978, Misar offered a modular helicopter-delivered system that could be configured to drop 3,744 SB33 anti-personnel mines or 240 SB 81 anti-tank mines, or a combination of the two,[15] in a matter of seconds. Both mines had minimum metal content, an optional anti-handling component and were highly resistant to explosive clearance methods. Helicopter delivery offered even greater speed of laying minefields in areas of air superiority and did not need an extensive logistics organization to transport mines to forward areas.

Italian mines in the 1980s were something of a phenomenon, with over forty different designs, many of them extremely sophisticated. They had a distinctive style incorporating highly resilient plastic casings and very precise plastic interior workings. Most mines are purely functional, but to the Italians form was important too. The mines featured textured plastic, with bold ribs and colour-contrasting pressure plates, doubtless the influence of Gucci and Armani shining through. The designs worked well for their export-orientated approach and many mines were bought by countries in the Middle East (with sand-coloured plastic) and in Africa and South America (with green plastic). Between 1976 and 1994 they exported a declared over $150 million worth of mines.

Other countries could use vehicles and helicopters to scatter mines but delivery by fast jet and by artillery fell to the US as part of a highly ambitious mine-warfare programme known as FASCAM (family of scatterable mines), which also included helicopter and ground-launcher delivery systems. The genesis of FASCAM lay in the Italian Thermos bomb and the German SD2 bomblet of the Second World War. The SD2 was copied by the US and the concept was further developed in the 1960s with a range of scatterable mines used in Vietnam. The FASCAM anti-tank mines had smart fuzes and full-width attack capabilities with shaped charges that were capable of destroying any armoured vehicle. The anti-personnel mines had a fragmentation effect initiated by tripwires that deployed on landing. All FASCAM mines included a self-neutralization mechanism with a maximum life once deployed of fifteen days, but they could be set for as little as four hours. Should the self-neutralization mechanism malfunction they could be rendered inoperable by the irreversible rundown of their batteries.

Caltrops attached to boards, recovered by Allied troops from German trenches in the First World War. The Caltrop has been used, practically unaltered, for 2,000 years. (*Imperial War Museum*)

Mine detectors were hastily produced during the Second World War. The first effective mine detector was designed by Polish Lieutenant, Józef Kosacki. This picture is of a production facility in South London during 1943. (*Imperial War Museum*)

During the campaign in North Africa both sides used prodigious numbers of mines. The Allied soldier on the left is holding an Egyptian Pattern (EP) anti-tank mine (which were considered 'dangerous to lay and even more dangerous to lift'); the one on the right holds a Polish mine detector. (*Royal Engineers Library, Chatham*)

An Egyptian Pattern mine recovered from Egypt over fifty years after it was laid.
(*Colin King*)

is pilot vehicle was improvised in the Western Desert in 1941 to locate the first row of mines in
vance of a deliberate clearance operation. The concrete-filled rollers were pushed ahead of the
hicle which was operated from inside an armoured cylinder. The technical notes claimed that
rivers of pilot vehicles are subject to considerable strain of a peculiar nature'. (*Royal Engineers Library,
tham*)

painting by Terence Cuneo depicting the breaching of the minefields at El Alamein on 23/24
tober 1942. It was no easy task, a British officer noted, 'we tried for the first time to use what were
led ''Scorpions'' [flail tanks] ... and they were very unreliable ... they broke down and got in the
y and then the Sappers had to [clear the minefields] by hand'. (*Royal Engineers Library, Chatham*)

Prisoners of war were often used to clear minefields. Afterwards, they were 'allowed to satisfy themselves that the ground had been thoroughly searched by walking over in close order'. (*National Army Museum*)

The Soviets laid millions of mines during the Second World War, sometimes under fire immediate in front of a German advance. This Soviet Sapper is digging in a wooden anti-tank mine at the Bat of Kursk. (*Imperial War Museum*)

An Allied advance in North-West Europe delayed whilst the route is checked for mines. During the Second World War mines accounted for 4 per cent of all personnel casualties and 25 per cent of all tank casualties.
(*Royal Engineers Library, Chatham*)

A German *Sprengbombe Dickwandig* 2kg (SD2), one of the earliest cluster munitions. The US copied the SD2 and used them in Korea and Vietnam.
(*Colin King*)

No. 1 Dog Platoon, Royal Engineers in Northern France in 1944. Dogs were, and continue to be, used to support some demining operations, but they have a variety of limitations. In the foreground the large wooden box is a *Holzmine 42* anti-tank mine, the large mines are *Tellermine* 35s, the rectangular boxes with the corrugated tops are captured French anti-tank mines and the white cones are mine markers.
(*Imperial War Museum*)

A German POW prepares to destroy a *Tellermine* 42 in Norway. Tens of thousands of POWs were employed as deminers after the Second World War. In Norway alone, 192 were killed and a further 275 were wounded. (*Imperial War Museum*)

Since the Second World War over 500 different types of mine have been produced. But far more effort went into designing and laying mines than into ways of countering them, leading to a widespread, long-term problem of uncleared mines in many parts of the world.

A truck after hitting a guerrilla mine in Mozambique. The driver was killed. After the war in Mozambique 30 per cent of the road network could not be used because of the threat of mines.

A Soviet POMZ anti-personnel fragmentation mine. The mine detonates when the trip wire is pulled; the fragments from its 'pineapple' body are explosively projected and can be lethal at up to 50 metres.

Soviet anti-tank mines. Clockwise from the top left: a TM46 with a tilt rod, a TM 46, a TM57, and a TM62, all with pressure fuzes. The mines have between 5kg and 7kg of high explosive and the TM62 could be fitted with a magnetic-influence fuze.

The French Minotaur mine-scatterable, anti-tank mine system (similar to the US FASCAM) can lay a minefield in a few minutes. The mines can also be scattered from 155mm artillery shells. The mines are cylindrical with a highly destructive shaped-charge warhead. They have a magnetic-influence fuze, an anti-handling device and self destruct after between one and ninety-six hours.

A French Armoured Engineer Vehicle fitted with full width mine plough, electromagnetic duplicator, rocket-propelled line charge and mine marker systems. The threat of mines created a demand for a wide range of countermeasures.

The German Khron demining system featured a soil mill that rotated counter to the direction of travel. The machine on the left is a plough used for quality control. The search for demining's silver bullet continues.

Racks of Soviet PFM1 'butterfly' mines. Thousands of these were dropped by aircraft on Afghanistan. (*Colin King*)

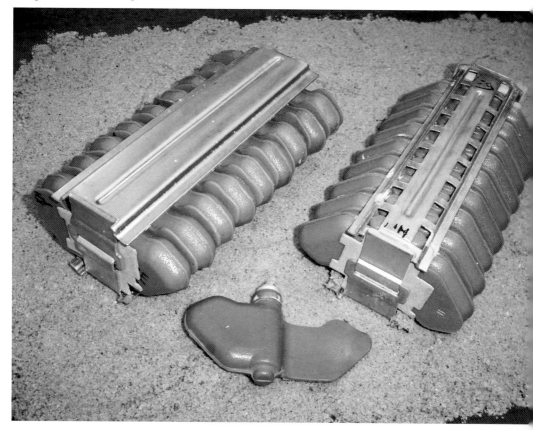

e US Hornet wide-area mine can attack targets up to 100 metres away. Targets are identified by smic and acoustic sensors; the device is then launched and uses an infra-red sensor to track the get which is engaged with its Misznay Schardin warhead. (*Colin King*)

ockpiled mines in Iraq. In the foreground are Soviet PMN anti-personnel mines, in the ckground Italian VS 1.6 anti-tank mines. (*Richard Boulter*)

Princess Diana brought worldwide attention to the mines issue. (*Richard Boulter*)

Amputees in Cambodia. Tens of thousands of civilians became casualties of mines long after the war had ended. (*Richard Boulter*)

A villager in Afghanistan with Italian VS50 anti-personnel mines that he had recovered close to his home. (*Richard Boulter*)

A dog handler in Rwanda. (*Colin King*)

Deminers at work in Afghanistan. They are spaced 20 metres apart to reduce the risk of multiple casualties. The work is invariably hot, dirty, boring and dangerous. (*Richard Boulter*)

Excavating a PMN anti-personnel mine which is buried about 15cm below the surface. Mines are normally blown in situ once located. (*Richard Boulter*)

demining team at work in a Sri Lankan orchard. (*Richard Boulter*)

Cambodian-built and operated Tempest mini flail. The Tempest is used for removing vegetation d preparing the ground for demining. (*Colin King*)

A Cambodian deminer using a dual-sensor mine detector which combines a sensitive metal detector with ground-probing radar, reducing the numbers of false alarms and speeding up the demining process. (*Richard Boulter*)

A deminer clearing agricultural land around a village in Cambodia. The stakes in the foreground indicate whe mines were found. (*Richard Boulter*)

Another member of the FASCAM family is the 'minefield in a suitcase' M131 modular mine pack system. This contains seventeen-anti tank and four anti-personnel mines, closely related to other FASCAM mines. The packs can be laid by hand individually or in groups of up to fifteen operated by a radio-controlled unit. On activation the mines are ejected up to 35m from the pack. If they are not activated, the pack can be removed for reuse. Another hand-emplaced mine, is the M93 Hornet. This device was designed to attack vehicles within a 100m radius. It contains acoustic and seismic sensors that detect and classify a target, so it has the ability to detect moving vehicles and discriminate, based on the engine noise, between enemy and friendly tanks. It then launches into the air, and another sensor tracks the target and fires a warhead through its turret. Both the M131 and the Hornet provide rapid, accurate emplacement with highly sophisticated detection capabilities, requiring only twenty mines over a kilometre of front, compared with 600 Barmines to cover the same area.

FASCAM represented a remarkable leap forward, providing the capability of creating minefields at any point on the battlefield, extremely rapidly, as part of intensive manoeuvre warfare. The mines were much more expensive than their conventional counterparts, but savings in logistics efforts and manpower helped to offset this. No longer was it necessary to transport mines from a logistics base to the front and get dozens of men to dig them in by hand – minefields could be laid in a few seconds, by a single pilot. They were not confined to ground occupied by US forces, but could lay minefields on top of enemy supply routes or assembly areas, thwarting any planned attack for just a few hours if necessary, providing tremendous flexibility for manoeuvre warfare. The system depended on excellent command, control and communication, with information about minefield location and duration needing to be disseminated in real time. But such was the flexibility of FASCAM that the US Army's greatest concern, stated in their field handbook, was that they 'offered an easy solution to tactical problems ... indiscriminate use of the weapon will result in the depletion of a unit's basic load'. In other words, they were so good that they might use them all the time and

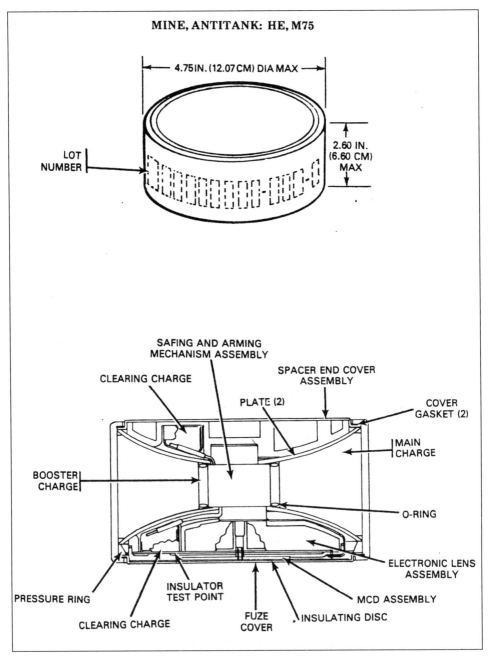

MINE, ANTITANK: HE, M75

A M75 FASCAM anti-tank mine with a magnetic influence fuse and highly destructive shaped-charge warhead.

therefore run out of supplies. To prevent this happening, by the end of the 1980s the US had around 19 million FASCAM mines in their arsenal. The delivery of FASCAM, together with new ground-attack aircraft and the development of artillery rounds that could sense tanks and attack them from above,[16] provided a range of options for resisting any armoured attack. It was an extraordinary transformation of defensive capability.

Fortunately it was never put to the test in Europe. Its first operational use was in the First Gulf War of 1990–1991. With its open, tankable terrain, lack of natural defensive lines and very large opposing armoured forces, an El Alamein-type encounter seemed plausible. The Iraq Army was competent and had years of recent fighting experience against Iran. To defend against a Coalition invasion the Iraqis developed a series of impressive minefields supplemented by oil-filled anti-tank ditches and wire entanglements. They used a variety of modern, mostly Italian, mines which were laid in depth and were covered by direct and indirect fire. They appeared a formidable obstacle and many in the Coalition were very concerned about how they might negotiate it. Minefields and other field defences had been extremely important in determining the outcome of battles in the Iran-Iraq war and they looked set to do the same in Kuwait.

It came as a surprise that the formidable-looking Iraqi minefields were breached in less than an hour using mine ploughs fitted to tanks, with comparatively small losses. In the breaching operation, US forces lost nine out of eighteen vehicles lost in the ground war, and twenty-nine out of 136 troops killed in ground combat – 50 per cent of vehicle casualties and 20 per cent of personnel casualties. This was a high proportion compared with previous wars, but it also reflects the lack of other weapons systems used by the Iraqis. The larger issue was why were the Iraqi minefields so ineffective? First, as articulated by the British Forces' Commander, General Peter de la Billière, the Iraqis, 'developed a defence based on the infantry intense Iran-Iraq war and not designed to stop or defeat massed armoured formations'. Secondly, Coalition forces spent a long time planning how they could breach the defences – they mobilized the appropriate equipment and executed the manoeuvre with well-rehearsed precision, with the support of overwhelming fire support from the ground and the air. US forces did however conclude after the war that they had limited means to counter mines away from the main minefields, so had they encountered scatterable mines or defended minefields, any breach would not have been so easy. Lastly, the Iraqis had been subjected to one of the greatest aerial barrages ever endured by defending troops, which sapped them of the means and the will to fight. The consistent lesson of minefields is that they are only effective if actively defended.

FASCAM was used for the first time in the Gulf War and demonstrated the additional capability provided by scatterable mines. Around 900 artillery delivery mines were used to cover gaps in advancing Coalition columns, and over 117,000 air-delivered mines[17] were dropped to disrupt supply routes, close airfields, interdict Scud missile launchers and to hinder the retreat of the Iraq Army. Frustratingly for such a recent conflict, there is very little hard information available on the casualties that they caused or their influence on the battle.[18]

The air-delivered mines were Gator BLU 91 anti-tank mines and BLU 92 anti-personnel mines. The presence of unexploded Gator mines was highly apparent across many parts of Kuwait immediately after the war. The failure rate was much higher than anticipated, with up to 2 per cent of the anti-tank versions and up to 20 per cent of the anti-personnel version did not function as designed. This was far higher than the 0.001 per cent failure rate demonstrated in trials. The most probable reason for this is that the collision of mines in the air, and the blast effects of other mines and munitions once they hit the ground, disrupted the electrical circuits.

The Gulf War turned out to be a mismatch between highly sophisticated forces and what were in comparison, solidly agricultural forces using out-of-date equipment. The imbalance neutralized the utility of the Iraqi minefields and masked the effects of the FASCAM deployment, so a note of caution should be added to any conclusions. What is clear, however, is that FASCAM represents a revolution in mine warfare providing capabilities previously unimagined. Had the threat of Soviet invasion of Western Europe materialized, it was a capability you would have wanted on your side.

Pressure

Pull

Tension release

Pressure release

Vibrations

Magnetic influence

Frequency induction

Audio frequency

Timer rundown

Electrical

There are many types of initiation mechanisms for mines.

Notes

1 This, I suspect, was because that unless their location is known to friendly troops, it is very easy to initiate tripwire-operated mines accidentally. The British Army did retain tripflares (a pyrotechnic rather than explosive device initiated by a tripwire). I set up quite a number when I served with the British Army; almost all were accidentally initiated by our own forces. I imagine there were similar problems with the Mark 2, with deadly results.

2 The Bazooka was one of the earliest anti-tank rockets, first introduced by the US in 1942. It has gone through many variations. Its name comes from its resemblance to a comical musical instrument played in the US in the 1930s.

3 Off-route or side-attack mines function using one of two basic principles: high-explosive anti-tank (HEAT) rockets incorporating a shaped charge, or a Misznay-Schardin plate which produces a self-forming projectile on detonation. Both have similar ranges (up to about 40m) but the HEAT rocket generally penetrates a greater thickness of armour.

4 Chief of the Defence Staff 1985–9, writing in Lieutenant Colonel C.E.E. Sloane's insightful Mine Warfare on Land, Brassey's, 1986.

5 In the soldiers' lexicon: 'build it, blow it, leg it'.

6 A kiloton is equivalent to 10,000 tons of TNT. For comparison, the Hiroshima bomb was about 12 kilotons and Nagasaki about 20 kilotons.

7 The information was declassified on 1 April 2004. Asked if it was an April Fool's joke, a National Archives representative told the media that 'It does seem like an April Fool but it most certainly is not. The Civil Service does not do jokes.' It's original code name was Blue Bunny – which would have made the whole story even more suspect.

8 National Archive, AVIA 65/2065. Interim instruction on the Nuclear Mine, 1955.

9 In the late 1980s, full-width attack fuses were developed.

10 Practice versions of the Ranger and Barmine, made respectively of peat and cardboard, were used by the Royal Engineers. During the 1970s and 1980s, training grounds across the UK and Germany were covered with them.

11 The Soviets copied this mine and, designated as the PFM1, used it in great numbers in Afghanistan.

12 Gravel mines were between 25mm and 89mm across, and 10mm deep, containing between 10 and 27 grams of a RDX/TNT mixture. Their designations included XM22, XM41 and XM 65. Details from Jane's, 2004–5.

13 The shaped charge is described on pages 58–9. To simplify some of the technical aspects I have continued to use the term for more modern shaped charges, which are more correctly referred to as 'Misznay-Schardin charges'; they are flatter than 'Monroe effect' shaped charges and thus easier to design into a mine, but still create an explosively formed projectile capable of penetrating great thicknesses of armour.

14 Valsella was half owned by the Italian car giant FIAT.

15 The SB33 and SB81 were used by Argentinean forces in the Falklands.

16 This was the M712 'Copperhead' artillery launched, fin-stabilized, laser-guided, explosive projectile that uses a laser-guided system to locate its target.

17 Around 2.2 million mines were taken to the Gulf for use by US forces.

18 A US General Accounting Office report for the House of Representatives on landmine use in the Persian Gulf War stated that the Department of Defense had not supplied information on the effects on the enemy. It is not clear whether the DoD would not disclose the information or did not have it. Given the level of disclosure about the US mines arsenal, I suspect the latter. Others may disagree.

Chapter 8

Guerrilla Mining

—⚊—

The Viet Cong successfully substituted mines and booby traps
for artillery.
Lieutenant General John H. Hay, 1974

That mines are defensive weapons, laid to create barriers to slow down attackers, has been true since the beginning of formal warfare. However, the late twentieth century saw the rise of guerrilla armies which used mines not to defend their positions, but to attack a stronger, organized enemy. From the second half of the twentieth century mines became an increasingly common weapon of guerrilla warfare. Guerrillas and mines are a potent combination – both cause disruption out of proportion to their numbers, and are difficult to locate and neutralize. Mines were used by Russian and Yugoslav partisans during the Second World War, with some success, to disrupt the German occupation forces. In Vietnam the technique of guerrilla mining was refined, becoming so effective that General Norman Schwarzkopf believed that some US units were 'so demoralised by landmines and booby traps that they had lost their will to fight'. The US dropped millions of scatterable mines across Vietnam with little, if any, military advantage to show for it. By contrast, the Viet Cong used a small number of well-placed mines to cause 70 per cent of vehicle casualties and 30 per cent of personnel casualties, creating widespread fear and disrupting operations throughout the country.

The Viet Cong had three sources of mines: those supplied by Communist governments; those they retrieved from US minefields; and those they manufactured locally. The Communist-supplied mines included the Soviet anti-tank mines, the wooden TMB D and the metal-cased TMB 2 and TM46, the Chinese No. 4 and the East German PM60.[1] Recovered US mines included the M16 'Bouncing Betty', the M14 'Toe popper', the Claymore and M15 and M21 anti-tank mines. US army figures from 1968 show that 16 per cent of Viet Cong mines (and 39 per cent of Viet Cong booby traps) located by US troops had been lifted from US minefields. Australian forces encountered similar problems. Of 20,000 mines laid to defend their positions in Phuoc Tuy Province, half were removed by Viet Cong infiltrators; the Australian Task Force Commander estimated that between 1968 and 1970 50 per cent of his casualties were caused by their own mines that had been reused by the Viet Cong. The Viet Cong essentially used minefields as ordnance depots. They also converted unexploded ordnance into mines, most commonly from US BLU 24 and BLU 66 cluster bombs. These were steel spheres about the size of a cricket ball and designed to fragment into small pieces when the explosive filling detonated. Once recovered they were fitted with new fuses, attached to tripwires and were known as the P-40 or apple mine.[2]

The Viet Cong also copied a variety of mines in small workshops dotted around the country, using skills learnt by their Viet Minh predecessors, who made mines for use against the French. Mild steel or cheap plastic were used for casings, and explosives were recovered from unexploded ordnance and melted into moulds of the appropriate shape; fuse mechanisms were normally very basic spring-loaded strikers retained by a pin attached to a pressure plate or a tripwire. This cottage industry underlined the simplicity of mines, much of their effectiveness was inherent in their concealment rather than their sophistication.

In the absence of conventional front lines, and with the Viet Cong able to blend in with the local population, surprise was one of their greatest assets. They could strike at US forces and slip away to avoid fighting set-piece battles against superior weapons. The largely unsealed road network was an ideal target. The Viet Cong would let convoys use a route for a few days. They would then plant a mine and scatter metal objects along the route to hamper efforts to locate it with metal detectors, before repeating the process at a different point on the road. These tactics were very effective at causing casualties and slowing down US operations. For example, from June 1969 to June 1970, the 11th Cavalry encountered over 1,100 mines. Only 60 per cent were detected; the other 40 per cent accounted for the loss of 352 combat vehicles.

To counter the threat a comprehensive approach was needed to stop mine laying, detecting mines that had been laid, and protecting men and vehicles. To prevent mines being laid US forces set up an informant programme, rewarding civilians for indicating the location of mines. It was not a great success as the fear of the Viet Cong was often greater than the desire for reward. A more successful tactic was aggressive patrolling aimed at preventing guerrillas getting close to roads. Ground-emplaced, motion-detection systems were also used, but the best way to avoid mines being buried was to seal the road with asphalt. It was not, however, totally effective as the Viet Cong would tunnel from the side of a road to plant mines under the asphalt, or use command-detonated mines placed in trees on verges. In response, many miles of road verges were cleared of vegetation. On other routes where it was not feasible to lay asphalt the tracks were sometimes sprayed with oil or paint to make any activity on the route immediately apparent.

Detecting buried mines was always challenging. The most effective method, accounting for a quarter of all mines located, was the trained eye, looking for disturbed ground, footprints on verges or the unusual absence of civilians in possible ambush sites. Mine ploughs were used in some areas, but these damaged the roads so badly that wheeled vehicles found them impassable. Rollers were introduced in 1969 but they were never entirely satisfactory. Armoured units disliked the reduced mobility that the 20-ton devices imposed, on soft tracks the rollers got stuck, and they often needed to be replaced after hitting a mine. Dogs were sometimes used but they were slow, easily bored and not always effective. Metal detectors were even slower, but they were useful for investigating any suspect areas. Mines continued to elude US forces who were forced to clear almost the entire Vietnam road network every day.

To protect against mine blasts, troops took to placing sandbags and flak jackets on the floor of their vehicles, especially M113 armoured personnel carriers and the new Sheridan light tanks, which were especially vulnerable to mine blasts. Such was the fear of mines that soldiers of the 1st Squadron, 1st Cavalry placed so many sandbags in their vehicles that they broke the transmissions on fourteen vehicles in forty-five days through overloading. Many soldiers rode on top of their vehicles, preferring to risk being blown off than being blown up inside. Belly armour kits were eventually issued for M113s and Sheridans, but nervousness persisted.

Footpaths were also mined by the Viet Cong so US soldiers were encouraged to avoid them and cut through bush rather than risk injury. This was slow and often impractical. One alternative, and to many the classic image of the Vietnam War, was to use helicopters to transport troops high above mine–ridden roads and paths. Helicopters could only land in cleared areas and inevitably these were targeted by the Viet Cong mine layers. Early anti-helicopter mines were simply hand grenades with their pins removed and tightly wrapped with paper which would hold in the grenade's fly-off lever. The downwash of the helicopter rotors would blow off the paper, allowing the fly-off lever to detach and leaving the grenade to detonate. The Viet Cong later produced a bespoke anti-helicopter mine with a main charge inside a cast-iron or concrete fragmentation jacket scored on the outside to look like a plant. A fuze was attached to two horizontal tin plates, specially shaped and painted to look like leaves. The downwash would depress the plates causing the mine to detonate. To avoid the threat, US forces used massive bombs to blow landing zones in thick jungle so they could be sure of landing without detonating a mine.[3]

Mines accounted, proportionally, for two or three times as many vehicle casualties in Vietnam as they had done in previous wars, and about ten times as many troop casualties. These striking figures in part reflected the Viet Cong's lack of air force, artillery or armour, but they also demonstrated the extent to which mines were used to take the fight to US forces. Mines proved extremely difficult to counter and absorbed huge levels of US resources. No single piece of equipment or tactic reduced the threat to any significant degree, the initiative always remained with the Viet Cong and mines were a serious threat throughout the war.

The next major guerrilla war to feature the widespread use of landmines was in Rhodesia, where the black majority fought for liberation after the white minority had unilaterally declared independence against hostile world opinion in 1965. Guerrillas used bases in neighbouring Mozambique and Zambia to attack Rhodesia. To prevent infiltration, the Rhodesians laid an extensive barrier minefield along the borders, initially 180km long but later extended to 850km, containing an estimated 2.2 million mines. The Rhodesians claimed that it was the longest man-made defensive line after the Great Wall of China.

Subject to international sanctions, Rhodesia was forced to manufacture its own mines, producing a tripwire-operated fragmentation mine and a copy of the British No. 6 Carrot mine, which was little more reliable that its original. The minefield lacked depth, and rainwater runoff exposed many of the mines enabling the guerrillas to negotiate the minefield safety and recover mines for their own use. Large sections of minefield were not fenced and were consequently open to wild animals which set off as many as 30 per cent of the mines. Sun-bleached animal bones paper chasing through the bush were a common indication of the presence of mines.

The minefield was a huge investment, but it served to underline that minefields only function to the extent that they are actively defended. The Rhodesians recognized that minefields could provide economies in manpower, which is why the barrier minefield was laid initially, but it still needed to be guarded. A guard force of say ten men per kilometre over that distance, working twelve-hour shifts, would require 17,000 troops. Rhodesia had 5,000 regular troops and a further 20,000 part-timers – it was therefore impossible for them to commit two thirds of their force to the task and consequently the utility of the minefield was extremely limited.

The guerrillas were, however, able to use a few mines with spectacular success. With no ground to defend, they had no need for barrier minefields; instead, they aimed to deplete the resources of the Rhodesians and undermine their will to fight by using mine-warfare tactics similar to those used in Vietnam (and in neighbouring Mozambique), with such success. Guerrillas were supplied with Soviet mines, mostly TM 46 metal-cased anti-tank mines. A common technique was to plant them on the approach road to isolated farms. A small group of guerrillas would then engage the farm in a firefight. The farmers would call for support and as security forces drove out to assist the farmer they would detonate the mine.

The first mine attack in Rhodesia was in 1972. From then until the end of the war in 1980 there were 2,504 mine attacks, killing 632 people and injuring 4,410. The rate of mining increased throughout the war, peaking in 1979 with an average of almost six attacks a day. It was a serious situation for the Rhodesians and they appeared to have few options to counter the threat. They did not have the resources to seal the roads, while ploughs, flails and rollers were slow, high maintenance and impractical in variable Rhodesian road conditions. If the Rhodesians could not prevent the attacks, they reasoned, they could lessen their impact by protecting the vehicle occupants. In unprotected Land Rovers, 44 per cent of vehicle occupants were injured in mine attacks and a further 22 per cent killed. To improve survivability they began filling tyres with water rather than air, as it absorbed some of the blast and reduced the heat of the explosion. The interior was protected with steel deflector plates, sandbags and rubber conveyor belting. This halved the fatality rate but still left many of the occupants injured. Attempts had been made during the Second World War,[4] Vietnam War and the Cyprus emergency to provide vehicles with mine protection with very limited success. It seemed unlikely that Rhodesia could provide a solution, but surprisingly it did, spawning an enduring world lead in mine-resistant vehicles by South Africa, a close collaborator in the endeavour. Their focus was on wheeled vehicles which, perhaps counter-intuitively, provided better protection from buried mines than tracked vehicles. Explosives are most effective when in close contact with a target, so vehicle tyres, and the higher crew compartments of wheeled vehicles, provided a critical stand-off distance. This was a helpful coincidence for the Rhodesians as they had very few tracked vehicles which are in any case more expensive, slower, and more difficult to maintain.

The major breakthough came with the adoption of the V-shaped hull, strong enough to deflect a blast, leaving the occupants unscathed if they were securely strapped in. The first mine-protected truck was the Hyena and the improvement in survivability rates was striking. Of 140 trucks that struck mines, only two of the 578 occupants were killed. But the injury rate remained relative high at 21 per cent and the vehicle was normally unserviceable afterwards.

The next stage in development was the Leopard, designed by Ernest Konshel, which used a monocoque construction. This meant that the engine and crew compartment were contained within a single hull with the axles mounted externally. A mine could destroy the wheel and axle leaving the rest of the vehicle unscathed, and the damage could be repaired relatively quickly and cheaply. The monocoque principle was applied to other vehicles – the Cougar, Ojay, Kudu and Puma – helping to reduce the casualty count and preserve its stock of vehicles which was especially important in a country subject to international sanctions.

Reducing the effects of mine blasts was a major step forward, but it did not solve the more fundamental problem of locating mines before they did any damage. Sweeping the long African roads with a hand-held metal detector was far too slow, so they reviewed the experience of vehicle-mounted detectors that had been attempted, with limited success, in other countries. There were two basic problems. First, on unsealed road there were often a surprising number of metal fragments (ring pulls, screws, silver paper and pieces of wire) that made detectors alarm. In Rhodesia they were fortunate that, initially at least, the guerrillas used large metal anti-tank mines, and metal detectors could be desensitized, enabling them to discriminate between large mines and small pieces of trash metal. Second, vehicles needed to stop before they ran over any mines encountered, which meant that a vehicle had to drive very slowly and the driver needed excellent reactions. The Rhodesians came up with a highly innovative solution: they mounted large detectors on a monocoque vehicle fitted with extra-wide racing car tyres, spreading the weight so it could not activate a mine. The vehicle was known as the Pookie and in four years of operational service they located 550 mines, losing only a single operator.

The Pookie's success made it a target for the guerrillas who frequently mounted ambushes against them. More effective, at a stroke neutralizing the Pookie, was the substitution of metal anti-tank mines with wooden-cased ones. The Rhodesians responded by developing a detector based on differentiating between soil densities. It was apparently used towards the end of the war with a degree of success, but it came too late to have much of an impact.

Mines were the major military tactic employed by the guerrillas in Rhodesia. They did mount ambushes, but infrequently and rarely on a large scale or in a particularly aggressive manner. Mines paralysed many parts of the country and imposed a severe strain on the Rhodesian forces. The most commonly highlighted aspect of mine warfare in Rhodesia was the innovations in mine-resistant vehicles. The key message, however, was that mining roads was an extremely effective guerrilla tactic.

The Soviets in Afghanistan had no more success than the US or Rhodesians in countering the guerrilla mine threat. The Mujahadeen mined routes between defended settlements, combining mine attacks with ambushes, the mountainous terrain lending itself well to this style of attack. A mine on a road in a valley would immobilize the lead vehicle and stop the following convoy. Often the road verges were also mined to prevent vehicle crews from finding cover. The Mujahadeen would fire on the convoy from neighbouring mountain tops, well protected from Soviet return fire. It was a very effective tactic and in parts of Afghanistan entire convoys of burnt-out Soviet vehicles were a common sight even years after the war ended.

The Mujahadeen commonly booby trapped mines to thwart clearance efforts. Against roller tanks, one of the Soviets' favoured clearance methods, the Mujahadeen would link a pressure-operated anti-tank mine to a large explosive charge. The charge was buried 3 or 4m from the mine in the direction from which the Soviets would approach. The rollers would pass over the charge and hit the mine which would detonate along with the charge under the belly of the tank. To counter prodding for mines, an electrical countermeasure was sometimes used. Two pieces of wire gauze were buried parallel to each other a few centimetres apart, and linked to a battery and an electric detonator. A metal prodder passing through the gauze would complete the circuit and set off the charge.

The Soviets countered the threat in much the same way as the Americans, by improving the protection for vehicles and their crews, aggressive patrolling, regular route clearance and dropping scatterable mines on likely ambush positions.[5] This mitigated the threat, but it did not eliminate it and mines accounted for up to 40 per cent of all Soviet casualties.

More recent conflicts in Afghanistan and Iraq have spawned guerrilla, or asymmetrical warfare as a viable and highly effective means of opposing occupying armies. One of the major tactics of the guerrillas (or insurgents) has been the prolific use of the roadside bomb or IED (improvised explosive device) which have claimed more than half of the Coalition casualties in each theatre. Many attacks are in urban rather than rural areas, and the devices themselves have sophisticated means of operation and considerable destructive power. This is a development of guerrilla mining and bears many features of mine warfare witnessed in Vietnam, Rhodesia and Afghanistan in the past.

In Vietnam and Rhodesia, long unsealed roads surrounded by thick vegetation offered a target and cover for guerrillas. In much of Iraq, however, flat ground with scant vegetation makes guerrilla operations in rural areas conspicuous and, with many of the main routes sealed, laying mines is difficult. Urban areas provide a much more profitable battleground for guerrillas, providing physical cover, a wide variety of target areas and a population amongst which to hide. Because it is difficult to bury mines in a hard environment, guerrillas have built roadside bombs. At first these were essentially large blast bombs made from salvaged munitions such as artillery shells, but they soon developed into highly destructive devices employing shaped charges (or explosively formed projectiles – EFP – as they are commonly termed in Iraq). This is essentially the same weapon that is used in modern anti-tank mines, and can be made very simply by filling a large pipe with explosive and placing a detonator at one end with a concave copper disc at the other. On detonation the copper disc turns into a slug of molten metal capable of piercing armour from several metres. The initiation system is made from a radio-controlled device or a mobile phone, and is operated by observers watching as a Coalition vehicle passes the device. When Coalition forces responded by introducing radio jammers to block the initiation signal, the guerrillas changed the initiation mechanism to passive infra-red sensors (similar to those used in home security alarms) that could not be blocked. The devices are often concealed in fibreglass casings designed, quite convincingly, to look like rocks. These provide insurgents with a 'drop and pop' capability – they can be placed on the side of the road and made operational in a matter of seconds.

Conventional mines have incorporated new technology, a FASCAM Gator mine, for example, is much more sophisticated than its predecessor, the round, pressure-operated, anti-tank mine; yet it remains a mine in both function, form and tactical use. In much the same way guerrillas' mines have incorporated new technology to produce what are termed roadside bombs, but they are essentially off-route mines. They are very similar to modern off-route mines (for example, the Russian TM83, German PARM2 and Polish Kasia 100) which combine passive infrared initiation with shaped-charge warheads. The guerrillas' mines may be improvised, but they are produced in large numbers and with sufficient consistency to be considered mass produced.

These devices pose a serious threat to Coalition forces, not least because of their particularly devastating effects. Mitigating the threat demands the same comprehensive approach that was used in Vietnam, Rhodesia and Afghanistan, including surveillance, intelligence, aggressive patrolling, detection and protection of men and vehicles. In urban environments where there are high levels of metal, electronic detectors have limited use, but new technology, using laser-induced breakdown spectroscopy, has shown some promise at detecting explosives at ranges of up to 30m. A major focus for Coalition forces is protection, this being one of the few areas where they can achieve demonstrable return on the investment. Troops now wear helmets and high-grade body armour for all operations as a matter of routine. For vehicle protection many forces look to what are now called Mine Resistant Ambush Protected (MRAP) vehicles as the solution. Their design is closely based on the Rhodesian and South African vehicles of the 1970s. The latest generation of MRAP vehicles include V-shaped or monocoque hulls to protect against blasts from the ground, with additional side protection against off-route mines, and top protection from overhead threats, such as rocket-propelled grenades (RPGs) fired from roof tops. This requirement comes at a time when many question the long-term requirements for tanks and tracked armoured vehicles which tend to be heavy, expensive and unsuited to the new forms of threat in guerrilla warfare. One of the largest military procurement programmes of the early twenty-first century is by the US Army and Marine Corps to acquire around 20,000 MRAP vehicles at a cost of $10 billion, which will replace most of the ubiquitous Humvee light vehicles[6] and some of the armoured fighting vehicles used in Iraq and Afghanistan.

Guerrilla mining has become much more sophisticated in recent years, and has adapted to urban environments. It remains a highly potent means of waging war and Coalition forces have been unable to suppress it, despite their comprehensive approach. The threat is no easier to counter in 2008 than it was in 1968. In most respects it runs counter to the concept of mines being defensive weapons. Indeed many would consider the guerrilla mine or the roadside bomb, a terrorist weapon. But to freedom fighters they are an entirely legitimate weapon to defend against a stronger occupier. Either way, the struggle between guerrilla mining and occupying forces looks set to continue, with past experience suggesting that the mine will not be defeated.

Notes

1 The TMB 2 was an early Soviet metal-cased, anti-tank mine, copied from an early Finnish anti-tank mine, which was also copied by the Germans as the *Holzmine 42*. The TM 46 is one of the most commonly used post-Second World War anti-tank mines, made of pressed steel with a simple pressure fuse. The Chinese No. 4 was an anti-tank mine which could also be set with a tripwire in the anti-personnel role. The PM60 was a minimum-metal mine.

2 The failure rate of the cluster bombs must have been very high. I saw dozens, perhaps hundreds, of P40s in Cambodia seventeen years after the end of the war, used not only as mines but also warheads for RPGs.

3 The bomb used was the 'Big Blue 82' BLU 82 which weighed 15,000lb and could clear a landing zone 75m wide.

4 In Tunisia in 1943, General Patton witnessed a demonstration of a mine-protected vehicle with a goat tethered inside. The official report noted that 'the goat died bravely.'

5 They used the PFM1, a copy of the US Dragon's Tooth that had been used in Vietnam.

6 High Mobility Multipurpose Wheeled Vehicle – HMMWV or Humvee as it is better known – was introduced in the 1980s to replace the Willy's jeep of Second World War fame.

Chapter 9

Humanitarian Mine Action

—ɷ—

Hundreds of thousands – perhaps millions – of people,
many of them children, have lost their lives, their legs, their
arms or their eyesight from stepping on landmines.
                                                    Senator Patrick Leahy

B y the 1980s, mines were firmly established in arsenals worldwide with over 500 different designs in service. Beyond military circles there was very little interest in mines and they had virtually no public profile. Mines had been used in great numbers during the Second World War and the tens of thousands of civilian casualties that they caused after the war were accepted with great stoicism. The great post-war demining efforts in Europe had largely been forgotten, although small numbers of mines and other explosive remnants of war (ERW)[1] continued to be discovered many years after they were laid. The end of the Cold War in 1989 also precipitated the end of many intra-state conflicts in the developing world that were sponsored by the superpowers. This provided opportunities for humanitarian groups to assess the needs of war-torn countries. In Afghanistan, Cambodia, Mozambique, Angola, Somalia and Nicaragua it soon became apparent that mines affected many aspects of life: they blocked roads, prevented farmers from planting crops, inhibited refugees returning, hampered rebuilding efforts and in particular, they caused large numbers of civilian casualties.[2] How did these modest weapons of defence turn into what some saw as weapons of mass destruction in slow motion?

The roots of the problem lay in the Cold War during which the Soviet Union provided military assistance to many developing countries and the US supported opposing guerrilla movements in what became protracted intra-state conflicts. Guerrillas typically launched small-scale surprise attacks against government-held key infrastructure (bridges, dams, ports, airfields and roads) and towns, avoiding being drawn into fights with stronger forces. To defend against these attacks, tanks, aircraft and artillery had little utility as guerrillas seldom presented a target, and in the developing world, heavy military equipment was difficult to maintain, required a high level of training and logistical support, and was expensive to operate. Mines, however, could deter attacks, required very little training to lay, needed no maintenance and were very cheap.

By the 1980s, the Soviets alone had over fifty different types of mine in service and a doctrine that encouraged their use in large numbers. Mines were exported to the developing world, where they provided a neat solution to the problem of guerrilla attacks. The presence of mines around a town or bridge displaced attacks to locations without mines, which generated an insatiable appetite for mines around every potential target. They rapidly became the weapon of choice in intra-state conflicts where they were described as the perfect soldier: standing guard in all weathers, with no need to sleep or eat, and with no need to be paid, yet they struck fear in the hearts of their enemies.

Most Soviet mines supplied to the developing world were simple but effective – what they lacked in sophistication they made up for in sheers numbers.[3] The most common type of anti-personnel pressure-operated mines were the PMD 6 wooden box mine (a copy of the German *schu* mine), the PMN (a large Bakelite-cased mine) and the PMN2 (a plastic-cased, blast-resistant mine). Tripwire-operated fragmentation mines included the POMZ[4] (a heavy cast-iron copy of the German *Stockmine*), essentially a large grenade mounted on a wooden stake, and the OZM series of bounding fragmentation mines. One common feature of all these mines was that they incorporated a 'safe-to-arm' mechanism.[5] This provided up to thirty minutes from setting the mine to it becoming operational, a useful safety feature, especially for poorly trained troops, ensuring fewer casualties when laying.[6]

Guerrillas also used the same offensive road-mining tactics that were so successful in Vietnam and Rhodesia, planting anti-tank mines on the long dirt roads so common in the developing world. Government troops would respond by planting anti-personnel mines along road verges at likely ambush points, and guerrillas laid mines on the approaches to sympathetic villages to inhibit aggressive patrolling by government troops. After years of conflict it seemed that everywhere was mined.

Mines offered people who had no real aggressive instincts the opportunity to defend their land, at little risk to themselves. Western armies had been killing en masse at close quarters for centuries, but people in the developing world did not have the same martial tradition. For them the mine was an ideal weapon – defending, not attacking, maiming, not killing – a weapon that allowed the substitution of the aimed shot for the random footfall. The chance nature of stepping on a hidden landmine seemed to integrate naturally with their superstitious traditions. In Buddhist Cambodia, if someone trod on a mine it was an act of fate rather than an act of aggression and soldiers tattooed themselves with images of mines to ward off the bad karma that might draw them to step on one.

Aside from the cultural differences, there were crucial practical differences between Western and developing world armies: the educational standards of soldiers, the level of training they received and the robustness of internal procedures – specifically the recording of minefields. To compound the problem, during protracted intra-state conflicts, troops were frequently rotated through garrisons or guard posts, often laying additional mines, so the size of the minefields grew, but the knowledge of their boundaries and their contents shrank. Often there was nothing available to fence or mark minefields, or if there was, such was the shortage of materials, it was stolen for use in house construction or to make stockades for animals. All armies, with the notable exception of the Germans, had historically proved ineffective at recording minefields, so it was hardly surprising that developing countries emerged from decades of conflict without minefield records.

At the end of the various intra–state conflicts, countries were impoverished, food was scarce, the security situation remained tense, hundreds of thousands of refugees longed to be resettled and mines started to take their toll. In war, movement is restricted and mines demark front lines which are normally avoided by civilians. In peacetime, when movement is much freer, the impact of mines, especially those laid around settlements and on roads, was profound, affecting many aspects of post-war life. As Afghanistan emerged from Soviet occupation there were over 3,000 mined areas covering over 850 square kilometres. After the war in Mozambique, half the entire road network was unusable due to the threat of mines.

The most striking impact of mines was the casualties. Wounds caused by any weapon are disturbing. All weapons, from hand grenades to artillery shells, are designed to kill by forcing metal fragments through human flesh at tremendous velocity, slicing, rupturing and breaking as they transit a body. The point where these fragments (shrapnel) enter the body is quite arbitrary and the wounds they inflict can range from slight to lethal. In contrast the wounds caused by pressure-operated, anti-personnel mines are remarkably consistent and instantly recognizable – the traumatic amputation of one or both legs. With reasonable medical intervention these wounds, although very serious, are not normally fatal. This is no accident, but a cynical equation designed to incapacitate soldiers, making them a burden on their armies. In the post-war developing world, mine victims were often agricultural workers, for whom the loss of a leg inevitably meant the loss of a livelihood and marriage prospects, and an additional burden on their fragile communities. Unlike other weapons that stop firing after a conflict, mines continue to kill and injure for many years afterwards. During the early 1990s it was thought that perhaps as many as 20,000 civilians were killed or injured annually by mines worldwide.

The end of the intra-state conflicts in the developing world coincided not only with the end of the Cold War, but also the end of the Soviet Union which had supplied and encouraged the mass use of

Pen & Sword Books

FREEPOST SF5

47 Church Street

BARNSLEY

South Yorkshire

S70 2BR

DISCOVER MORE ABOUT MILITARY HISTORY

Pen & Sword Books have over 1500 titles in print covering all aspects of military history on land, sea and air. If you would like to receive more information and special offers on your preferred interests from time to time along with our standard catalogue, please complete your areas of interest below and return this card (no stamp required in the UK). Alternatively, register online at www.pen-and-sword.co.uk. Thank you.

PLEASE NOTE: We do not sell data information to any third party companies

Mr/Mrs/Ms/Other...............Name..

Address..

....Postcode...................

Email address..

If you wish to receive our email newsletter, please tick here ❑

PLEASE SELECT YOUR AREAS OF INTEREST

Ancient History	❑	Medieval History	❑	English Civil War	❑
Napoleonic	❑	Pre World War One	❑	World War One	❑
World War Two	❑	Post World War Two	❑	Falklands	❑
Aviation	❑	Maritime	❑	Battlefield Guides	❑
Regimental History	❑	Military Reference	❑	Military Biography	❑

Website: www.pen-and-sword.co.uk • Email: enquiries@pen-and-sword.co.uk

Telephone: 01226 734555 • Fax: 01226 734438

the mines. The Soviet Union bears a heavy responsibility for the mine problem throughout the developing world, where most mines laid are of Soviet origin, yet Russia has been conspicuously absent from the lists of countries providing practical or financial assistance to tackle the problem.

The principle established after the Second World War was that countries cleared mines on their own territory with little outside help (apart from prisoners of war). Demining was often undertaken by military units soon after hostilities ended, as occurred in Europe and Korea. In some countries mined areas were not cleared because they remained militarily sensitive (i.e. Israel), or had little value (i.e. Egypt's Western Desert), there were no resources for demining (Zimbabwe), or due to particular technical difficulties (i.e. the Falklands).[7] Unusually for a poor country, Vietnam cleared large areas of mines and unexploded ordnance using its own resources and only accepted small-scale international assistance in the late 1990s. In Kuwait around 5 million mines were cleared following the First Gulf War by commercial contractors at a cost of $800 million.[8] But this stands as a rare example of a country being able to afford its own large-scale and rapid clearance operation. Some might suggest that the developing world would not address its own mine problem because the West, motivated by humanitarian values or liberal guilt, would inevitably take on the task. But the reality was that the developing world's litany of problems was so great and its resources so limited that international assistance was absolutely necessary.

The response to the multi-faceted problems caused by mines developed into five main pillars: assistance to mine victims; mine risk education; mine clearance; stockpile destruction; and a process to ban the production and use of mines (the ban on mines is the theme of the following chapter) in a $500 million a year worldwide mine-action programme. Its genesis lies with the International Committee of the Red Cross (ICRC) which was amongst the first to recognize the problems caused by mines and to provide assistance to mine victims. This assistance is provided at four levels: first, surgery to treat the wound and help it heal; second, prosthetic limbs to help amputees to regain mobility; third, vocational training for amputees; and finally, the promotion of rights and opportunities for the disabled. The ICRC has operated prosthetic workshops in Afghanistan, employing mostly disabled staff, under the guidance of Alberto Cairo, an Italian prosthetics expert, since 1989. In Afghanistan there are over 50,000 mine accident survivors, in Cambodia around 45,000, and in Angola around 60,000. Other international NGOs providing assistance to victims include Handicap International and the Cambodia Trust, which run prosthetics workshops in mine-affected countries where the need is not just for a single prosthetic limb following an accident, but replacement limbs every couple of years as the old ones wear out. So the demand for assistance endures throughout the life of a mine casualty.

Providing assistance to the victims of mines is clearly an essential part of mine action. However, preventing people from becoming victims is far preferable, and mine-risk education aims to do that by informing people about the dangers of mines and the locations of mined areas. People become mine victims in one of two ways: they handle mines, or they stray into minefields. People handle mines to move them to a safer place, or out of curiosity; an impulse all too common in children, often with tragic endings. People stray into minefields unwittingly as they are often unmarked, or out of necessity because they need access to land to tend crops or to collect firewood. A study in Cambodia in the early 1990s showed that 73 per cent of mine victims knew they were entering a mined area but decided to take the risk. When working in Cambodia I came across a boy of ten or twelve whose cow had strayed into a minefield. I told him not to go after the cow. He stared at his feet for a long time then looked at me, tears streaming down his face, took a deep breath, ran into the minefield and beat the cow until it trotted back to safe ground. The boy too returned safely, but he had clearly calculated the risk to himself and his cow and was well aware of the consequences of his gamble.

Mine risk education is designed to raise awareness of the risks resulting in behavioural change and therefore fewer accidents. It is best achieved by a combination of public information campaigns and community education programmes. Typically this may include radio broadcasts and travelling performers who stage plays or traditional shows about the dangers of mines. In 2006, direct mine-risk education (not mass media) was delivered to over 7 million people in forty-three countries. Mine-risk education is provided by local NGOs in mine-affected countries, with ICRC, UNICEF and the Mines Awareness Trust active internationally, as well as demining and mine victim assistance organizations providing education in parallel with their core activities. I like to think that with mine-risk education the Cambodian boy's instinct for self-preservation might have been keener.

Assisting victims and educating people about the risk of mines is necessary, but only demining can eliminate the risk and is the most important aspect of any mine action programme. The genesis of humanitarian demining lies in the United Nations (UN) sponsored Operation Salaam of 1987–9 which brought together foreign military engineers to train Afghans to demine in the expectation that they would return to Afghanistan and clear mines. After training 13,000 men it was recognized that deminers needed not only training, but equipment, vehicles, administrative support and especially money, if they were to run a successful operation. In 1989, the UN switched its focus from purely training and started to coordinate demining on the ground. The previous year the HALO Trust, a British charity, started clearance work in Afghanistan, and by 2007 was, by some way, the largest, employing 9,000 deminers in nine countries. Started by Colin Mitchell, a former high-profile officer in the British Army, HALO has remained very focused on the task of removing the debris of war and thrives in challenging environments. Other international NGOs include the Mines Advisory Group, which is also British based, Norwegian People's Aid and the German Menschen Gegen Minen. Many of the leading commercial demining companies are British and a significant number of senior mine-clearance appointments in the UN are held by British nationals.

The British domination of demining is a result of various factors. Most people involved in demining are former soldiers and the British Army has long experience of mine warfare, leading back to before the Second World War. It is also one of the few professional armies with a tradition of overseas service, often working closely with local people. The frontier soldiering feel of running demining operations in remote parts of the world appeals to the romantic adventurous spirit of many former soldiers. A sizeable cadre of British soldiers gained first-hand experience of mines through attachments to UN demining programmes in Afghanistan, Cambodia and elsewhere, or on operations in the Falklands, the Gulf War and in the Balkans. The downsizing of the British Army as part of the post-Cold War peace dividend encouraged many to look for new challenges in civilian life. British firms won several major commercial demining contracts in Kuwait after the Gulf War, in part because of the British Army's contribution to the liberation of Kuwait. The dozens of ex-British soldiers working on the contracts were the most experienced deminers available at around the time that humanitarian demining took off. Added to that, the strong international NGO sector in Britain was keen to work closely with demining agencies in war-torn countries and found a pool of seasoned experts willing and available to work. The British Government, long a major donor to overseas aid projects, was a strong supporter of demining, and British NGOs and commercial contractors were best placed to access these funds. So history, first-hand experience and a ready supply of money combined to ensure that British deminers were able to provide leadership in humanitarian demining worldwide.

The demining world is small, with perhaps 200 expatriates active in the field. The joke has it that deminers are either mercenary (in it for the money), missionary (attempting to do some good in the world) or misfits (running away from something or someone). Like most jokes there is an element of truth in it, although many expatriate deminers fit into more than one of the categories. Wages are between $50,000 and $100,000 a year, but the cost of living in, say, Angola is very cheap so most deminers are able to save a good proportion of their (often tax-free) salary. But they have to work hard, leading a Spartan existence in hostile conditions, facing difficult technical and managerial challenges, and shouldering responsibility for large numbers of indigenous deminers and for the safety of communities who use demined land. Most have a genuine commitment to the countries they work in, striving to improve the lives of mine-affected communities. Often they have a fascination with mines, spending hours dismantling, reassembling, photographing, cataloguing and drawing them. There can be few deminers who have not returned home on leave without some mines (with the explosives removed) tucked into the recesses of their rucksacks to place on their mantelpieces. Most deminers' homes are stuffed with technical pamphlets, mine warning signs, prodders, exploders, ammunition tins, shell cases and dozens of mines – the paraphernalia and trophies of their trade.

Deminers tend to downplay the risks of their work. Whilst only a small handful are killed or injured annually, either by mines, road accidents, disease or as victims of crime, before long the list of friends and colleagues whose luck has run out starts to grow. So it is not surprising that after a few years at the sharp end of demining, jobs in international demining administration, based in New York, Geneva or Washington, start to look attractive.

The 20,000 or so indigenous deminers working across the world seldom get the opportunity to work internationally. They too are generally former soldiers recruited as they were demobilised from their rag-tag armies. There is no shortage of volunteers to become deminers, with regular employment the key motivator. In the developing world, where large proportions of the population subsist on what they can grow, a wage of $200–$300 a month, paid in dollars, is highly attractive. In addition to the wage they can also expect routine medical care, annual holidays, a uniform and often the reassuring presence of a kindly expatriate manager. In return they spend forty-eight weeks a year living under canvas in demining camps, many miles from home, doing a dirty, boring and dangerous job.

Demining NGOs tend to work on long-term programmes with a strong humanitarian focus, while commercial companies tend to work on shorter-term projects, often with a financial rather than humanitarian focus. For example, an NGO might work to clear low-value agricultural land whereas a commercial company might clear land for the extension of an oil terminal, although in reality the distinction between commercial and humanitarian demining can be somewhat hazy.

Since 1988, demining has transformed from an unregulated, small-scale activity to an international business with several layers of bureaucracy and a set of international standards which regulate how it is conducted. At a national level demining is coordinated by mine action centres, or MACs. MACs bring together information on mined areas, casualties, socio-economic impacts, and use it to coordinate demining and mine-risk education. They provide a focal point for lessons identified, statistical data, quality assurance and the application of international mine-action standards. Above the MACs a number of international organizations have assumed responsibilities for aspects of mine action. The UN provides a focal point for policy coordination, funding and resource mobilization, with fourteen UN departments having a role in mine action. The Geneva International Centre for Humanitarian Demining studies operational issues and disseminates information. James Madison University in the US acts as an information centre and publishes a *Journal of Mine Action*. The Survey Action Center, again in the US, coordinates impact surveys. The Landmine Monitor reports on compliance with the 1997 mine-ban treaty and assesses the international community's response to the humanitarian problem caused by landmines. Mines are cleared to a set of international standards that form the benchmark for running demining operations, mine-risk education, surveying minefields, testing equipment, ordnance disposal, using machines and dogs, and a variety of related aspects of mine-action programmes.

The various organizations cooperate with each other, but not always with great affection. NGOs compete with each other for funding and are suspicious of commercial demining companies which believe that NGOs ruin the market for commercial activities and are held to lesser performance indicators. Both NGOs and commercial companies are frustrated by national MACs which they see as bureaucratic, corrupt and poorly equipped to coordinate their activities. MACs find NGOs and commercial companies unwilling to be coordinated and lacking in transparency. People working at national level and in the field consider the various international organizations remote, bureaucratic and of limited relevance (although they might jump at the chance to work for them). It is a complicated web of relationships.

Whilst the bureaucracy surrounding demining has grown markedly, the techniques are little different to those employed after the Second World War, and demining remains depressingly slow. Demining in 2008, like that in 1948, depends on a sharp eye, a sharp stick and a sensitive metal detector. Demining teams can range from six to forty strong, with deminers working individually in parallel one-metre-wide lanes about 20m apart to reduce the risk of multiple casualties if a mine is initiated. As in 1948, the deminer makes a visual search for mines immediately in front of him. He might use a length of wire to feel for tripwires and then pass a metal detector over the ground in front of him. If the detector alarms he investigates the ground using a steel prodder. If he locates a mine it will be excavated sufficiently to place an explosive charge alongside and it is blown up in situ. The essence of demining is very simple.

Most people, when asked to close their eyes and imagine a minefield, will conjure up an image of an area of short grass, a recently ploughed field, or a sandy desert surrounded by a neat barbed-wire fence with red warning signs every few metres. Unfortunately the reality is very different. Minefields in the developing world are often covered with a tremendous tangle of vegetation and are seldom fenced. It is sometimes said that searching for mines is like looking for a needle in a haystack, but finding the haystack, or at least tracing its boundaries, can be a considerable challenge itself.

In the absence of records or fences, minefields are located using a variety of sources. Hospital statistics are a good starting point as they may provide information on the cause of injuries and where they were sustained. Survey teams then visit towns and villages to ask about the war-time history, mine casualties (both human and animal) and land-use patterns. Lastly, surveyors look for visual clues to indicate the presences of mines. An overgrown field is a classic indication of a minefield. In some areas villagers knot long grass or place crossed branches on the ground to indicate the presence of mines. Animals sometimes stray into minefields and get blown up, their sun-bleached bones remaining to signal the hidden dangers. If lucky, it might be possible to see mines – perhaps the fuse of a fragmentation mine poking up through earth with tripwire attached, or the rim of a pressure mine exposed by soil movements. I have spent many hours peering into minefields for clues about the locations and types of mine, but it is the exception rather than the norm to actually see any trace, especially in heavily overgrown areas. Only a small part of the overgrown area may actually be mined, so to locate the mined area deminers clear into the thicket until the first row of mines is located. It is a painstaking task, but if done effectively it can greatly reduce the area needed to be cleared, considerably speeding up the job. In some areas, tired of waiting for demining teams, villages gradually cultivate land deeper and deeper into mined areas, stopping when they find the first mines, the overgrown strip between a chequerboard of cultivated fields clearly showing the minefield.

For a mine detector to be effective it must be operated very close to the ground, so the vegetation must be cut very short, taking care not to pull any tripwires, using a small pair of secateurs or shears. It is the equivalent of filling a bath a thimble at a time where spilling a drop may set off a bounding fragmentation mine. There has been some success in recent years using machines to cut vegetation in advance of demining operations. One successful design, pioneered by Menschen Gegen Minen in Angola, is a South African Casspir armoured vehicle (a refinement of similar vehicles used during the Rhodesian war), with a mechanical rotor for cutting vegetation. In Cambodia, a number of organizations operate a remote-controlled mini flail known as the Tempest which is produced in Phnom Penh by local staff, many of whom lost limbs to mines. These machines do not clear mines, but in overgrown areas where deminers can spend 80 per cent of their time cutting vegetation, they significantly accelerate the process. Recent models are fitted with a magnetic array that helps to reduce metal contamination. The Tempest is about the size and weight of a small car and can easily be transported around countries with poor infrastructure. Another way to speed up the vegetation-cutting process is to check first for tripwires and bounding fragmentation mines using a metal detector, then if clear, to use a hand-held petrol-powered strimmer to slice through the vegetation, which is then raked into a safe area, leaving the cleared area prepared for the detector to search for buried pressure-operated mines.

As well as vegetation, metal contamination makes demining especially slow and frustrating. In people's imaginary minefield, every beep of the metal detector indicates the presence of a mine, but the reality is that former war zones have vast quantities of bullet casings, shrapnel, silver paper from cigarette packets, nails, rusty buckets, pieces of wire and assorted items of scrap metal that are also identified by detectors. Plastic-cased mines contain very small amounts of metal, often little more than a pin head, so metal detectors need to be very sensitive if they are to locate mines, however this also causes them to alarm on the tiniest of metal fragments. Yet each alarm has to be treated as if it were a mine, the ground carefully probed, and the metal fragment identified and removed from the ground to prevent further false alarms. To put this in perspective, the Cambodian Mine Action Centre recorded 392,478 mines cleared between 1992 and 2008. During the same period, 386 million items of scrap metal were retrieved from mined areas. That means that for every mine found there were 983 false alarms. Demining is accompanied by the constant sound of metal detectors buzzing like crazed bees. Magnets can be used to attract metal fragments on the surface which reduces the number of false alarms, but the ratio remains at many hundreds of false alarms for every mine. In Cambodia in 2006, 4,000 deminers located 33,000 mines and 25 million metal fragments, so on average during that year alone each deminer found eight or nine mines and over 6,000 metal fragments.

In some areas metal contamination is so severe that it is easier to dispense with detectors, dig a trench around 30cm deep in a safe area and excavate into the minefield using an entrenching tool with a sideways motion, exposing any mines from the side without disturbing the pressure plate on top of the mine. It is hard physical labour, especially on sun-baked ground, but it is very thorough. The technique has been used to clear roads in Mozambique using gangs of local labour under the supervision of experienced deminers, and by the French military on the beaches of Kuwait.

Accidents commonly occur whilst probing for mines, or as a result of mines being missed by the detector and then trodden on by a deminer. The use of good procedures and absolute consistency are essential to minimize the risk of accidents, especially as the average deminer locates very few mines a year (in Afghanistan during 2006 each deminer located, on average, three mines) but investigates thousands of detector alarms.

Is demining any safer now than it was sixty years ago? Measured by the number of man hours worked, according to one study,[9] a deminer in 1945 became a casualty on average after every 890 hours worked, compared with Afghanistan in 1997 where the rate was one casualty for every 50,000 hours work. But if we compare casualties per mine cleared, the picture is somewhat different. During post-Second World War demining operations, casualty rates were in the region of one deminer killed or injured for every 2,000 mines cleared.[10] In Afghanistan between 1990 and 2006, eighty-two deminers were killed and 633 injured clearing around 360,000 mines. That is one deminer casualty for every 500 mines cleared.

After the Second World War deminers routinely cleared several hundred square metres a day compared with the modern deminer's 10–20 square metres. So deminers today work more slowly, but are at least as likely to have an accident. There are several important reasons why the risks remain high (demining is, by some way, the most hazardous occupation that can be insured) whilst the speed of clearance is much slower. Today's deminers are better trained and their equipment is more efficient, but the gap between mine–detector sensitivity and the metal content of mines has remained fairly constant over the past sixty years. The German *schu* mine of the Second World War was as difficult to locate using a Polish detector as modern minimum–metal mines are using the latest detectors. Perhaps the most significant difference between the eras is that after the Second World War many minefields were reasonably well marked and recorded, they were laid to predictable patterns, the mines were larger (thus easier to detect by prodder) and had often been in the ground for only a few months or up to a couple of years. The term minefield suggests a formality that rarely exists in the developing world, there are seldom records or discernable patterns and mines have often been in the ground for many years, with shifting or compacted soil and heavy vegetation adding to the difficulties. Modern humanitarian demining often resembles a cross between gardening and archaeology, with lethal consequences if mistakes are made.

Deminers today are equipped with prodding and excavating tools specially designed to deform rather than shatter in a blast. They wear a range of protective equipment including a helmet with a visor, a blast-resistant jacket or apron, and sometimes blast-resistant boots (which are only partially effective even on very small mines). So whilst demining remains dangerous, the severity of injuries to deminers can be reduced.

That demining remains hard physical labour is a source of immense frustration, prompting a search for the silver bullet – the perfect mine-clearance machine – a quest that began in 1918 when rollers were first attached to tanks. Rollers can breach lanes to assault through a minefield, but they are not sufficiently reliable and cannot clear whole minefields. Ploughs simply push mines aside. Flails can be rendered ineffective by uneven terrain and thick vegetation and some mines are designed to be flail resistant. Grinders, or earth tillers, use a steel beam with tungsten teeth to grind the soil and detonate or disrupt mines, achieving a higher rate of clearance than flails but sharing many of the same drawbacks. All demining machines have similar limitations: they are expensive, require considerable maintenance and logistics back-up, and they are difficult to transport around the fragile infrastructure of the developing world and most importantly they are unreliable. In the right conditions they can speed up the process, but they need to be supported by manual deminers. And machines are not always viewed as an appropriate solution in the developing world, as much of the cost of the operation remains in the West, whereas manual demining programmes employ large numbers of locals and their salaries help to stimulate a poor economy.

Dogs are sometimes used to support demining operations, but they too are not 100 per cent effective at locating mines. They need extensive training, careful handling and their performance varies.

Their main role is in identifying the extent of mined areas, but they need to be used intelligently if they are to justify their considerable expense.

The challenge of demining has attracted many inventive brains. Some of the more imaginative ideas have included low-flying supersonic aircraft to create an overpressure to detonate mines, divining for mines using a pendulum, using a hot-air balloon as a demining platform, sowing minefields with cress that grows on soil permeated with nitrogen from explosives, and training rats and bees to locate mines. Sadly none of these have proved practical and all too often they have been allowed to progress without their inventors or sponsors having any real understanding of the practicalities of minefields and demining.

One of the most promising innovations in demining has been the emergence of a new range of mine detector that combines ground penetrating radar (GPR) with a sensitive metal detector. The GPR is able to identify anomalies within the soil and, combined with the metal detector, it provides a high degree of confidence for deminers as well as speeding up search operations by reducing false alarms. The US Handheld Standoff Mine Detection System (HSTAMIDS) was first used operationally in 2006 and looks set to increase demining productivity. Recent trials in Cambodia showed that deminers we able to clear up to 200 square metres a day – a tenfold increase in productivity. For deminers it may not be the silver bullet, but it could be the wooden stake.

It takes about as long to clear an area of 100 mines as it does to clear it of five mines. It is the searching for mines that takes the time, not the disposal of them. Mines are usually blown up in situ using a small explosive charge (it is the single most satisfying moment in a deminer's day). The unit of measurement for demining productivity is not the number of mines cleared, but how many square metres are cleared. However, these figures can be difficult to interpret as there are essentially three types of clearance. First, there is demining or minefield clearance where progress is typically little more than 10–20 square metres per man per day. Second, there is area reduction, where an initial survey indicates that a large area is mined but a subsequent more detailed survey is able to reduce the area that needs to be cleared. So, for example, an area surrounding a village might be thought to be mined, but a detailed survey reveals that only one side of it is actually mined; the area is thus 'reduced' from the total that needs to be cleared without any physical clearance taking place. Third, there is the clearance of former battlefields which are not mined, but littered with unexploded ordnance. These are normally searched visually by teams of men spaced 10 metres apart, only using detectors in areas where ordnance might be buried. Battle area clearance (or BAC as it is known in the trade) can be undertaken relatively quickly with rates of clearance up to several thousand square metres per man per day. In Afghanistan in 2006, around 8,000 deminers cleared 26 square kilometres of minefield and 108 square kilometres of former battlefield, in addition to which 34 square kilometres of minefield were 'reduced', with 13,728 mines and 900,000 items of unexploded ordnance being destroyed during the various operations which cost $87 million.[11] In the same year in Cambodia, 4,000 deminers cleared 28 square kilometres of minefield and 'reduced' a further 17 square kilometres, destroying 36,745 mines and 113,000 items of UXO at a cost of around $30 million.[12] Not only is demining slow, it is also expensive, with the clearance of a single square kilometre of minefield costing the best part of a million US dollars.

In the early days of humanitarian demining the focus was on numbers of mines in the ground, which led to a long running and often heated debate within the mine action community. In Afghanistan, the first country to develop a mine action programme, the UN estimated that there were 10 million landmines. This figure had no analytical basis whatsoever but was to have significant repercussions as it was used as a benchmark against which other mine-affected countries were measured. In Cambodia, the next country to develop a mine action programme, the UN estimated that there were 7 million landmines as it was felt that Cambodia was not as heavily mined as Afghanistan. Mozambique was next with an estimated 2 million mines, then Angola, thought to be the most heavily mined of all, with 15 million. On went the estimates until a

UN report in 1993 claimed that 'the 110 million landmines buried world-wide will cost approximately $33 billion for clearance alone and at current rates of funding would still take more than 1,100 years to rid the world of mines now in the ground.'

Many parties stood to gain from high estimates of the numbers of mines. Mine-affected countries could generate more assistance, the International Campaign to Ban Landmines could generate more outrage, commercial companies could generate more contracts, and the media could generate a more sensational story. Some deminers appreciated that the figures were greatly exaggerated and were concerned that the 'Landmines, Damn Lies and Statistics'[13] controversy would make donors shy away from an issue that would take 1,000 years to solve – indeed there was some evidence of this in the early years of humanitarian demining.

In the late 1990s, the HALO Trust produced estimates of number of mines that were much lower than the UN figures: Afghanistan 400,000 to 600,000, Cambodia 300,000, Mozambique 250,000 to 300,000, Angola 500,000.[14] So who was right? In 2008, after almost twenty years of demining effort, well over half of the major minefields that impact human activity have been cleared and clearance programmes in many countries are essentially residual. It is surprisingly difficult to obtain figures for the number of mines cleared so far in many countries as the unit of measurement for demining has shifted from numbers of mines to square area. But it is easy to get a sense that the figures, once so heavily used by the UN and the ICBL, are now deliberately obscured. Numbers of mines cleared to date in the most heavily contaminated countries appear to be in the region of: Afghanistan 380,000, Cambodia 395,000, Mozambique 100,000, Angola 200,000. This suggests that at the final count the number of mines worldwide will be closer to 5 million than 110 million.

With the number of mines proving a distracting and confusing measure, square area was seen as more reliable. But here too there are difficulties with the figures. Estimates of areas mined are rarely accurately or consistently measured. In an attempt to address this, the US sponsored worldwide landmine impact surveys which aimed to provide consistent data, by which the mine problem could be quantified and prioritized. But the survey used such a loose methodology, applied by staff with insufficient knowledge of their subject, that it generated more heat than light. For example, a survey of Mozambique in 2001 estimated that 562 square kilometres required clearance. In 2005, a new survey revised this to 149 square kilometres (of which actual clearance accounted for only a small proportion of the decrease). In 2006, this was reduced further to 60 square kilometres, with some local officials suggesting that only a tenth of this might need clearance. In Kosovo, only 41 of the estimated 360 square kilometres required clearance. So whilst square area is a more reliable guide than numbers of mines, much depends on how an area is measured and who is doing the calculations.

Casualty data is a helpful gauge of a country's mine problem as preventing casualties is one of the key aims of mine action. The accuracy of data varies, but in recent years it has become reasonably reliable. There may be a degree of under-reporting in some countries, but in others casualties may be over-reportrd as mine victims are often singled out for special treatment (priority medical treatment, income support, retraining etc.). A Mine Action Support Group held a conference in Geneva in 2007, entitled, with no apparent irony, *Mine Action after Clearance is Complete*. Someone losing their leg on a mine may get lifelong support, whereas their neighbour who loses a leg in a road accident receives only basic medical treatment. So people who have lost limbs as a result of road accidents or infections often claim that they are mine victims to qualify for additional benefits. And in recent years, mine casualty figures have been broadened to include not just mine injuries, but injuries caused by all types of unexploded ordnance. Even so, the figures demonstrate that mine action is working. In the early 1990s, there were an estimated 20,000 mine victims (killed and injured) annually; in 2006 the figure was 5,751, with Colombia accounting for over 1,000 (mostly military) victims. In the same year in Afghanistan mines killed ninety-eight and injured 698, while in Cambodia mines killed sixty-one and injured 389.

There is no doubting the horrors of mine injuries, but as a public health issue, even in the worst mine–affected countries, they rank very low as causes of death. Road accidents account for around 8,500 deaths annually in Afghanistan and 2,800 in Cambodia. In low-income countries 1.5 million die annually from diarrhoea and nearly 2 million women die in childbirth. It is striking to make comparisons between malaria and mines, not least because they both mainly affect the developing world. Annually mines kill around 1,500 people and injure 4,500 others; malaria kills 1.2 million and causes sickness in 350 million others. Mine action attracts $500 million in funding annually; malaria action attracts $600 million annually (a shortfall of $2.6 billion of the total needed to provide universal malaria prevention and treatment). That is $330,000 for each mine fatality and $500 for each malaria fatality. The comparisons should not be stretched too far, not least because the area–denial aspects of the mine problem can be profound, but there are parallels between the two problems. Nevertheless, it is clear that mine victims can mobilize sympathy like few other groups.

So why does mine action attract proportionately so much more money than malaria? I think there are three key reasons. First, the West (the bulk of the aid donor community) feels a sense of guilt about mines, believing itself responsible for their presence and the casualties that they cause, whereas malaria is a natural phenomenon unconnected to the West. Second, images of mine victims are intensely shocking, leaving an indelible image, whereas images of feverish malaria victims do not have anything like the same impact. Thirdly, not only are the images shocking, they have been promulgated worldwide by the ICBL and platoons of celebrities and high-profile people, making mines an issue of worldwide public concern. This combination of guilt, shock and profile has ensured that the money keeps flowing.

Funding for mine action has increased steadily from around $100 million in the 1990s to $500 million in 2006, with the largest contributions provided by the US ($94 million) and the European Commission ($87 million).[15] Additionally, tens of millions of dollars are absorbed by demining research and development projects which have arguably contributed little to address the problem. Perhaps only half the money provided for mine action is used directly to get mines out of the ground. The frustrations were articulated by Guy Willoughby, the Director of the HALO Trust at a summit on a mine-free world in Nairobi in 2004, who suggested that the problem with mine action was that many in it

> seem content to encourage millions of dollars being spent not on mine clearance, but yet more endless working groups, workshops, information management systems, symposia, strategies, studies, standards, plans, policies, portfolios, principled programming, processes, procedures, quality management, mainstreaming, methodologies, measurables, monitoring, quality control, consultations, consultants, courses, conferences, capacity building – and the full range of outreaches, outputs, inputs, indicators, impacts, intervention logic, linkages, gendering, thematics, logical frameworks, normative frameworks, blockages, goals and supergoals.[16]

He made a good point: the ratio of deminers to demining administration and monitoring has decreased over the years and it is easy to get a sense that this burgeoning mine-action infrastructure has an interest in perpetuating the problem rather than ending it. The Nairobi Summit attracted heads of governments, Nobel prize winners, representatives of 135 states and 350 NGOs, yet its output was measured not by action, but by words.

It is illuminating to compare the modern humanitarian mine problem with post-Second World War demining operations. The size of the problem was certainly comparable, indeed in 1945 there were many more mines, probably over a similar area and affecting as many countries. Europe in 1945 faced many similar problems to the developing world as it emerged from conflict: limited equipment and money, food shortages (food rationing in Britain did not end until 1955) and ruined infrastructure. Despite these problems (or maybe because of them) the demining operations were organized with a high degree of pragmatism with tens of thousands of men mobilized (50,000 in France alone) and a determination to complete the job quickly. They succeeded in clearing 100 million mines in less than three years with small teams working over a longer period to clear residual problems. Had the experience been used as a template for modern humanitarian demining, progress would have been far greater. Instead, much more modest numbers of deminers have been employed for much longer periods: nearly twenty years in Afghanistan and sixteen years in Cambodia. This has perpetuated the problem, resulting in more mine casualties and greater expense. The 350,000 mines around the beaches of England during the 1940s caused around 500 casualties. The 300,000 mines in Mozambique have caused around 30,000 casualties. The lack of urgency in ending the mines problem is because there is a good deal of self-interest in seeing it sustained. Some believe that if the various mine-action bureaucrats, advocates, administrators and monitors were formed into demining platoons and marched off to Afghanistan and Cambodia, the mines problem would be solved in short order.

Notes

1 Explosive Remnants of War are essentially the same as unexploded ordnance – UXO.
2 One of the best accounts of the many problems caused by mines is Davies, Paul, *War of the Mines: Cambodia and the Impoverishment of a Nation*, Pluto Press, 1994.
3 Whilst most Soviet mines were very simple, in the 1980s and 1990s they developed a range of more sophisticated mines including an anti-tank mine with a Misznay-Schardin plate and a magnetic-influence fuze TM89), a helicopter scatterable anti-tank mine (PTM3), anti-helicopter mines (TEMP 20) and a top attack off-route mine (TEMP 30).
4 In the Soviet nomenclature 'O' means fragmentation, 'Z' means obstacle and 'M' means mine. A PMN is an anti-personnel mine, tread operated. PMD is an anti-personnel wooden mine. The best technical book on Soviet mines is Jefferson, Paul and Haywood, Lyn, *Warsaw Pact Mines*, Miltra Engineering, 1992.
5 The safe-to-arm mechanism was a model of simplicity, incorporated into the pencil-like striker housing. When the safety pin was removed, the spring loaded striker was prevented from operating until a wire loop at the back of the striker, under pressure of the spring, worked its way through a small strip of lead, allowing the striker to be retained by a second pin attached to a tripwire.
6 That said, even with this mechanism, laying mines can cause a degree of anxiety. I once laid a field of 320 Soviet anti-personnel mines (to test mechanical clearance equipment). Despite being an experienced deminer, and operating in a controlled environment, I was surprised to discover my heartbeat quickening every time I removed a safety pin after setting a tripwire or digging in a pressure-operated mine.
7 Around 16,000 Argentinean mines remain in over 100 minefields in the Falklands. The use of minimum-metal mines in shifting peaty soil proved a difficult combination. Demining commenced soon after the end of hostilities with assistance from

cooperative Argentinean PoWs, but after three casualties (two British, one Argentinean) were sustained in the first week of operations, it was decided to fence off the minefields as the land they were on was unproductive. A further two British troops lost legs on mines outside minefield fences in 1983, but no one has been injured since then.

8   There was a human cost too. Eighty-four contractors were killed and a further 200 injured during the clearance operation, and 1,700 Kuwaitis were killed or injured on mines or ERW between 1991 and 1995.

9   Lardner, Tim, *Study of Manual Mine Clearance*, GICHD, 2005.

10 This figure excludes Poland where casualty rates were unusually low, suggesting incomplete data.

11 Figures for unexploded ordnance cleared often need interpreting as they can include individual bullets. Cases of thousands of bullets are often abandoned on battlefields and are cleared much more easily than larger individual items of ordnance.

12 The figures are from The Landmine Monitor and the Cambodian Mine Action Centre. The costs also include those of the broader mine action programme, of which the bulk was for demining.

13 Deminer Paul Jefferson writing in the Guardian in September 1997.

14 These figures are from *120 Million Landmines Deployed Worldwide: Fact or Fiction* by Ilaria Bottigliero, published by Leo Cooper in 2000.

15 Other major contributions in 2006 came from: Norway ($34.9 million), Canada ($28.9 million), Netherlands ($26.9 million), Japan ($25.3 million), United Arab Emirates ($19.9 million), United Kingdom ($19.3 million), Germany ($18.6 million) and Australia ($16.5 million).

16 Speech given by Guy Willoughby in November 2004 at the Nairobi Conference to mark the five-year point after the Ottawa Landmines Ban Treaty was signed.

Chapter 10

Banning the Mine

—◊◊◊—

No exceptions, no reservations, no loopholes.
Jodie Williams, ICBL Coordinator

D eminers saw their task as getting mines out of the ground, but humanitarian workers believed that, because mines were indiscriminately killing and injuring civilians long after wars had stopped, they should be banned. Achieving this would be their task.

There were precedents for banning weapons. In the twelfth century, the Pope had banned the use of crossbows against Christians, while in 1675 a treaty between France and the Holy Roman Empire forbade the use of poisoned bullets. Moving into the industrial era, the Hague Convention of 1899 banned the use of expanding or dumdum bullets,[1] poisonous gas and bombing from the air (obviously with mixed success). Despite the widespread use of mines during and after the Second World War, there had been no attempt to ban or restrict their use, although the Third Geneva Convention of 1949 forbade the forced employment of prisoners of war for demining. It was not until after the Vietnam War that attempts were made to restrict the use of mines – it was the indiscriminate civilian casualties caused by the new scatterable mine systems in Vietnam that made the critical difference. This happened at a time when the unpleasant realities of war were seen for the first time by people on television, which in turn lowered the Western public's appetite for slaughter.

The International Committee of the Red Cross (ICRC) alerted governments to the development of mines and other weapons that they believed caused excessive injuries or had indiscriminate effects.[2] Their efforts to raise awareness of particularly nasty weapons coalesced into a United Nations conference in 1980, known as the *Convention on Prohibitions or Restrictions on the Use of Certain Conventional Weapons Which May be Deemed to be Excessively Injurious or to Have Indiscriminate Effects*, more usually referred to as the CCW. The CCW's *Second Protocol on Prohibitions or Restrictions on the use of Mines Booby Traps and Other Devices* prohibited their use against civilians, restricted the use of scatterable mines unless their location could be recorded, or they had adequate self-neutralizing mechanisms, and obliged states to record minefields and to clear them after the cessation of hostilities. The text provided the military with considerable latitude, for example Article 3 stated: 'All feasible precautions shall be taken to protect civilians from the effects of [mines] ... *Feasible precautions are those ... which are practicable ... taking into account all circumstances ruling at the time, including humanitarian and military considerations.*' And Article 5 stated: 'Effective advance warning shall be given of any delivery or dropping of remotely delivered mines which may affect the civilian population, *unless circumstances do not permit*' (my italics). Only forty-one states (mostly NATO and Warsaw Pact countries) signed the CCW, it did not apply to internal conflicts and there was no monitoring mechanism.

The final outcome of the CCW was a major disappointment to many who felt that military considerations had been given priority over humanitarian concerns. They were right, but in the context of the period it was about as much as they could realistically hope for. In 1980, the world was in the grips of the Cold War, and mines were viewed as defensive weapons that might one day save the West from a massed Soviet attack, which, following their invasion of Afghanistan in 1979, was a real issue. In any case, attempts to restrict the use of some weapons that were considered excessively injurious were completely overshadowed by negotiations to restrict the proliferation of nuclear weapons, known as the Strategic Arms Limitation Talks.

And the peace lobby were far more interested in banning the bomb than banning the mine.

The period between the end of the Cold War and the start of the War on Terror provided an opportunity to revisit the issue. The threat of nuclear war between the superpowers greatly receded, deflating the 'ban the bomb' movement. The end of the Cold War allowed humanitarian organizations, and soon after the wider world, to see the impact of mines on civilian communities. The thousands of limbless victims made it a moral issue that no military objective could justify. This was a cause which united the peace movement, humanitarian groups, politicians and a surprising number of soldiers to mobilize public opinion against mines. In 1991, *The Coward's War: Landmines in Cambodia*, published by Human Rights Watch (HRW) and Physicians for Human Rights (PHR), was the first study of the plight of mine-affected communities in UN-administered Cambodia.[3] Its final paragraph issued a challenge: 'The UN and the ICRC should consider an unconditional ban on the manufacture, possession, transfer, sale and use of landmines and other devices that detonate on contact in all international and internal conflicts.'

The following year a group of six NGOs – Handicap International (HI), HRW, Medico International (MI), Mine Advisory Group (MAG), PHR and Vietnam Veterans of America Foundation (VVAF) – agreed to coordinate efforts against mines and appointed as its coordinator, Jody Williams, a feisty activist from Vermont. The campaign became formally titled the International Campaign to Ban Landmines (ICBL) which encapsulated its message very clearly and concisely: ban landmines. What they meant was:

1. A complete ban on the use, production, stockpiling, sale, transfer or export of anti-personal mines.

2. Increased resources for demining and mine awareness programs.

3. Increased resources for victim assistance and rehabilitation programs.

Given the limited success of previous attempts at arms control this seemed fancifully optimistic, but these were interesting times. From its core group the ICBL grew organically, developing into dozens of national campaigns and supported by hundreds of NGOs worldwide. Taking advantage of new email communications, the ICBL gathered remarkable momentum.

In 1993, the campaign received high-level recognition when the UN General Assembly adopted a resolution calling for a moratorium on the export of anti-personnel mines. Soon afterwards the Swedish Armaments firm Bofors announced, for 'moral reasons', that it would stop manufacturing AP mines and, a month after a Vatican Council called for a ban on mines, Fiat announced the sale of its shares in the Italian mines manufacturer Valsala.

In 1995, Handicap International persuaded French President Mitterrand to call for a review of the 1980 CCW. This proved to be something of a setback for the campaign because, although it tightened up some of the original articles, the main revision was the legalization of self-neutralizing mines. Many armies thought self-neutralizing mines were the perfect compromise between military and humanitarian needs, allowing the use of mines that would deactivate themselves after predetermined periods, eliminating the threat to civilian communities and, as they were scattered on the ground rather than buried and had a very high metal content, were easy to recover after a war. But politicians disagreed and in the same year Belgium, a mine manufacturer and exporter, became the first country to ban the use of landmines, to be followed later that year by Switzerland, Canada and the Philippines.

A boost to the campaign came from an unlikely source. Fifteen retired US generals, including Norman Schwartzkopf, Commander of Coalition forces in the First Gulf War, wrote to President Clinton saying that a ban on mines would be 'human and militarily responsible', adding that:

> Given the wide range of weaponry available to military forces today, antipersonnel landmines are not essential. Thus, banning them would not undermine the military effectiveness or safety of our forces, nor those of other nations. The proposed ban on antipersonnel landmines

does not affect antitank mines, nor does it ban such normally command-detonated weapons as Claymore mines, leaving unimpaired the use of those undeniably militarily useful weapons.

General Wesley Clark, the Supreme Allied Commander Europe, took the other side in the debate, expressing his concern at the military consequences in a Congressional hearing: 'Self-destructing and self-activating anti-personnel landmines and anti-tank/anti-personnel mines systems constitute a critical force protection and counter-mobility asset.' President Clinton had been keen to support an end to anti-personnel mines but his serving generals argued that they were still needed in Korea (where thousands of mines helped to protect the South from attack) and that 'smart' (self-neutralizing or self-destructing) mines were not excessively dangerous to civilians. President Clinton's mine policy therefore developed into three main strands: an end to the use of 'dumb' mines by 1999 except in Korea; the continued use of 'smart' mines; and a leading role for the US in negotiating an international mine ban that was consistent with US policy. It was another disappointment for the ICBL.

Meanwhile, public awareness of the issue soared as the media developed a fascination for mines, and indeed it was an engaging story: grotesquely injured children, amputees begging in the street, prosthetic clinics, deminers sweating under the tropical sun, explosions, 4 x 4 vehicles, war, poverty, shady arms dealers, stout military types, indignant peace campaigners, politicians, the UN and the very many members of the public worldwide who felt strongly enough to make piles of shoes in their capitals to remind everyone that the war against mines was being lost one leg at a time. And then there were the statistics provided by the UN, which seemed almost biblical: 110 million mines buried worldwide, 26,000 people a year killed or injured, 1,000 years to clear all mines (which was, as we have seen in the previous chapter, something of an exaggeration). A photograph of a maimed child with the words 'Ban mines' was an extraordinarily powerful message.

The 'ban the mine' campaign did, however, have its dissenters, led by Paul Jefferson, from the UK and one of the leading deminers of the time, whose articulate message was especially powerful as, not only did he have expert knowledge of his subject, but also he had been blown up whilst demining in Kuwait, losing a leg and his sight in the process. Jefferson argued that the ban was drawing resources away from demining for two reasons: first, because the problem had been exaggerated so greatly that no one would fund it; and second, because a lot of money devoted to the mines issue was being spent on conferences, advocacy and raising awareness of the issue rather than getting mines out of the ground. He made a reasonable point: had the emphasis been on clearing mines, the work would have been completed much more rapidly and in the past ten or fifteen years, tens of thousands of people might have been spared the experience of treading on a mine. A 'ban the mine' campaign could have followed on from the 'clear the mine' campaign and we might have had the best of both worlds. But it is also important to remember that during the first half of the 1990s it appeared that more mines were being buried in Kuwait and the Balkans than were being cleared in the developing world, which suggested that clearance without a ban was a Sysipheon exercise.

The campaign's focus remained on a ban rather than on clearance, and despite disappointment about the outcome of the CCW and stance taken by the US, there appeared to be enough countries interested in a complete ban on anti-personnel mines to prompt Canada to invite both states and NGOs to Ottawa in 1996 to investigate how to take forward the idea. The Ottawa conference divided states into those who were interested in banning mines by the year 2000, and those that wanted observer status. The Canadians eventually agreed to drop the timescale in return for full US participation, but it was a temporary papering over of what was to develop into a significant crack. Canada had a long tradition of peacekeeping and international humanitarian action, but the US had international strategic interests and the use of mines played an important role in defending them. Banning mines was easy for the Canadians but not for the US. The conference proceeded unremarkably until the final day of the three days when, to everyone's surprise, Canadian Foreign Minister Lloyd Axworthy unilaterally announced that there would be another conference in Ottawa the

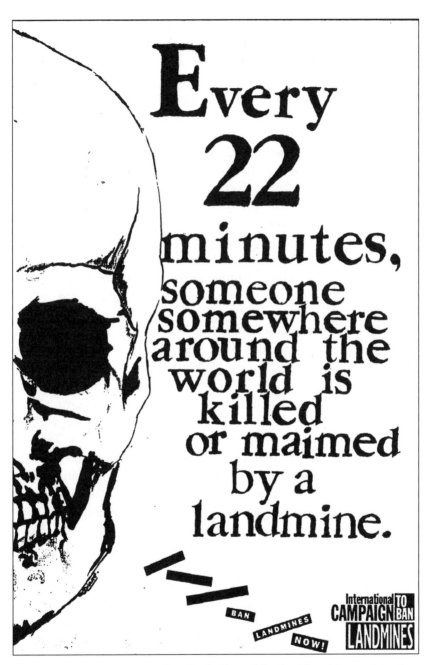

The International Campaign to Ban Landmines mobilized public opinion against mines.

following year at which countries could sign a treaty banning mines.

The announcement was met with elation by the ICBL but deep frustration by some governments. It was bad diplomatic form to surprise countries in such a manner and there was considerable unease about the role of NGOs in negotiating arms-control treaties. More seriously, it put the US in an embarrassing position. The US wanted to be part of a process for minimizing the impact of mines on civilians whilst preserving its strategic defence interests. Its publicly stated policy was not about to be overturned by a coalition of peaceniks and lightweight governments. The most President Clinton felt able to do was pledge that the US would destroy its stockpile of 'dumb' mines and commit the US to a reinvigorated CCW process. But the proposed mine ban treaty went several steps further than defence interests would allow and the US was forced to withdraw from the Ottawa process. Without the US there was little hope of getting Russia and China on board and any ban would have serious limitations.

In January 1997, soon after the first Ottawa conference, the campaign received a massive boost when Princess Diana, the most photographed woman in the world, lent her support to the cause by visiting minefields in Angola. This caused uproar in the British Government which at the time was inclined to retain anti-personnel mines, and a junior Defence Minister described her as a 'loose cannon'. Princess Diana's involvement took the mines issue from the inside pages of the broadsheets to the front page of the tabloids. Public opinion, and not just in Britain, swung behind the campaign to ban mines and developed an unstoppable momentum. In May 1997, a new Labour Government was formed in Britain and, brushing aside the previous Conservative Government's policy, announced that it would support the ban on mines. Princess Diana died in August 1997 and was remembered for her close association with the mines issue. One of the most enduring images is of her in an Angolan minefield wearing a HALO Trust blast-resistant vest. The small irony was that the HALO Trust was one of the few NGOs that was not involved in the campaign to ban landmines finding it a 'distraction' from its stated mission of 'getting mines out of the ground, now'.

The campaign gained official credibility and moral authority in spades when, in October 1997, 140 years after the Nobel family produced naval and land mines for the Crimean War, the ICBL and its coordinator Jody Williams were jointly awarded the Nobel Peace prize 'for their work for banning and clearing anti-personnel mines'. This generated a huge amount of excitement and anticipation for the forthcoming Ottawa conference, but proved highly controversial within the demining community and campaign alike. The idea that the award was in part for 'clearing' mines angered deminers who saw no evidence of the ICBL having cleared a single mine – indeed many thought it had actually set back mine clearance by several years, sensationalizing what was a practical task. Amongst campaigners the naming of Jody Williams was highly contentious. A number of individuals had played crucial roles in the success of the campaign: Rae McGrath, a passionate early advocate for banning landmines, who had also founded the Mines Advisory Group to address the practical problems of mines; Bobby Muller, founder of VVAF, a paralysed former US Marine, another early catalyst for the campaign, and the man who had employed Williams; Princess Diana who had prompted so much interest in mines; Lloyd Axworthy who laid down the challenge to governments to sign the ban treaty; Senator Patrick Leahy, the US Senator who had tirelessly lobbied to get US support for the ban. Any of these might have been contenders, however the feeling within the campaign was that it was not driven by any individual, but by a groundswell of public opinion.

The process by which Williams was also nominated was mired in controversy. The campaign's steering committee had agreed that 'the ICBL should be nominated with Jody Williams the individual who would be the recipient for the campaign.' So Williams would collect the award on behalf of the campaign, rather than be a co-nominee. In the nomination letter the words *on behalf of the campaign* were omitted and it was submitted to the Nobel Committee, not by the obvious choice, William's co-Vermonter and leading mines advocate, Senator Patrick Leahy, but by US Representative James McGovern, who had a long-standing working relationship with Williams. A few days before the announcement of the Nobel Peace Prize, Williams was fired by her employer VVAF, and to inflame the situation, Williams, in a break with tradition, announced that she would keep the $500,000 prize money. Since 1997, Williams has continued to work full time, apparently unsalaried, as an ambassador for the ICBL. It almost feels as if she is atoning for the peace prize controversy.

The internal controversy did not deflect the campaign from its course. The mine ban treaty or, as it was officially known, the Convention on the Prohibition of the Use, Stockpiling, Production and Transfer of Anti-Personnel Mines and on their Destruction (see Page 186), was signed in Ottawa on 3 December 1997 by 122 countries. Parties to the treaty agreed never to use, develop, produce, acquire, stockpile, retain or transfer anti-personnel mines, and also to destroy stockpiles (although some could be retained for training). The anti-personnel mines that were banned were those that were victim operated. Command-initiated anti-personnel mines, such as the Claymore, were permitted, as were anti-tank mines, even if they were fitted with anti-disturbance fuses (which made them liable to detonate if handled). In response to deminers' concerns, the treaty also provided a framework for the clearance of all buried mines with Article 5 obliging countries to fence minefields and to clear all mines in their territory within ten years of signing the treaty.

The treaty was a monumental achievement, the fastest and broadest piece of arms-control legislation ever introduced. By 2008, 155 countries had signed the treaty and compliance with Article 1, forbidding the use of mines, appears very high. Vast stockpiles of anti-personnel mines have been destroyed, often accompanied by some ceremony. In the mid 1990s, it was estimated that there were 260 million mines stockpiled in 130 countries; by 2007 these figures had dropped to 160 million mines in forty-six countries. Of fifty former mine-producing countries, thirty-eight have stopped production.

Thirty-seven countries have not signed the treaty, including the US, Russia and most former Soviet states, China, most Middle Eastern states and Finland, which used mines very effectively during the Winter War of 1939 and remains the only European country outside the treaty. Since the treaty was signed mines have been laid regularly by Russia and Burma, and on occasions by others including Eritrea, India, Iraq, Israel, Kyrgyzstan, Nepal, Pakistan, Sri Lanka, and Uzbekistan (all non-signatories to the treaty). However, only relatively small numbers of mines have been laid and there has been no return to the massed mine laying of the 1980s. The non-signatories are all countries with an active security threat where mines are retained as a useful means of defence. So the mine treaty essentially split the world into two: those peaceful countries that could afford to sign the treaty, and those with security threats that could not.

Mines have also been used by guerrilla groups, or what are now termed non state actors (NSA) in Afghanistan, Burma, Burundi, Chechnya, Colombia, DR Congo, India, Nepal, Philippines, Somalia, Sri Lanka, Sudan and Uganda. These groups are also non-signatories to the treaty, but there is no mechanism for them to sign and even if provided with one, they are unlikely to forsake mines.

The interesting question is: what mines might have been laid if it were not for the mine-ban treaty? The campaign can claim, with justification, to have stigmatized the use of mines, thus reducing their use and raising the threshold for deploying mines amongst non-signatories who value world opinion. Since the treaty was signed there have been no shortage of armed conflicts, but the style of modern warfare has created few circumstances in which mines might have been used. Most conflicts have been asymmetrical struggles between large conventional forces and much smaller guerrilla groups. There have been few front lines to defend and little need to surround military positions with mines as they offer no protection from vehicle-borne suicide bombers or incoming mortar rounds. It has been the guerrillas who have become the major users of mines, especially anti-tank mines, with neither group nor mine within the scope of the treaty. There is no doubt that mine use is much less than it was two decades ago, but in large measure this is because the changing nature of warfare has reduced the need for mines, rather than the treaty inhibiting their use.

Article 5 of the treaty called for minefields to be fenced and mines within them to be cleared within ten years of signature. The clause on fencing was entirely unrealistic and it is difficult for people in the West, especially those with no experience of mines, to understand why. As we saw in the previous chapter, tracing the outlines of minefields is difficult and dangerous. Fencing material is soon stolen in the developing world (and if it isn't, it needs regular maintenance). and remote minefields rarely need fencing. So the treaty has not precipitated the widespread fencing of minefields. There is, however, much talk about the other Article 5 requirement to clear mines within ten years of signing the treaty. It has been taken seriously by Denmark which in 1946 fenced off a German minefield in coastal dunes in Jutland. The minefield had not caused casualties in over fifty years and the land was of low value, yet to ensure compliance with the treaty a $16 million project was initiated to clear about one square kilometre of land. The UK is unlikely to meet Article 5 requirements over the Falkland Islands minefields and looks set to engage a caveat within the treaty to apply for an extension to the deadline. Until the treaty was signed, the expense and (technical difficulty) of clearing minimum-metal mines buried in shifting peaty soil was not considered worthwhile as the land was of little value and the mines were not affecting economic or social activity. The 20 square kilometres of Falkland Island minefields would cost millions of dollars to clear and would expose deminers to a significant risk, whilst achieving little more than ensuring compliance with the treaty. Of the heavily mine-affected countries, few are likely to meet their Article 5 obligations and will cite limited financial resources as the reason.

Another question in the demining fraternity is: for how long do mines remain fully operational in the ground. German Second World War mines are remarkably durable. Both metal and wooden anti-tank mines recovered buried in the dunes in Jutland in the twenty-first century were in perfect condition, with the painted lettering still quite readable. And the Norwegian Army was using captured German Army detonators, still quite gleaming, forty-five years after the end of the Second World War. But recent evidence from Cambodia suggests that Chinese and Russian plastic anti-personnel mines might not remain operational for as long as previously thought. Many mines are no longer capable of functioning due to the degradation of the detonators and the explosive charge, and because burrowing insects make homes in them. There is not sufficient evidence to suggest that you can walk risk free through old minefields, but you might get a second chance, and you might think twice about demining remote, low-value and low-impact areas containing mines that degrade.

Article 5 aimed to promote demining, but there is little evidence that it has generated new momentum to complete the task. In part, lack of impetus, as we saw in the last chapter, is because the demining world is riddled with bureaucracy and self-interest whilst devoid of analytical ability. Article 5 provides a useful and public measure of the amount of clearance needed, but it risks distorting the issue by insisting that countries demine marginal land, at increasing costs, for limited benefits.

The ICBL pursues its goal of a mine-free world, with universalizing of the treaty as its major aim. It zealously measures global progress against the treaty's various articles using an extensive web of agents, and publishes a 1,000-page annual report covering 118 countries.[4] It has maintained public interest in mines and continues to capture the imagination of a host of high-profile people including Queen Noor, Paul McCartney, Heather Mills McCartney, footballer David Ginola, Sheryl Crow and many others who raise money for landmine issues. The mines issue has an appeal that transcends a lot of other worthy causes.

Many involved in the ICBL are also pursuing a ban on cluster munitions which were first used in North Africa and England during the Second World War. Half a century later they have evolved into highly effective weapon systems which, when dropped from aircraft or delivered by artillery, detonate over a wide area to attack hard targets (armoured vehicles or protected buildings) and soft targets (human flesh). They also fail to function as designed on occasions. In Kuwait in 1991, I came across dozens of cluster munitions strikes, with the fins of unexploded bomblets sticking out of the desert like carrots in a field (for the technical, US Rockeye Mk 118s), and there are more recent examples of unexploded cluster munitions in Kosovo, Afghanistan and Lebanon. If they fail to function they assume the characteristics of landmines – they are not designed to be victim operated, but by virtue of their sensitive fuse mechanism are liable to detonate at the lightest of touches. It is for this reason that there is strong support, led by the Cluster Munitions Coalition, to ban these weapons. It looks set to follow the model created by the ICBL, with countries facing a security threat becoming non-signatories, but being more discerning in its use. The issue is not on the same scale of that of landmines. There are many fewer cluster munitions strikes, their high metal content and tendency to come to rest above ground make them much easier to locate and they cause far fewer casualties. Landmine Monitor claimed that there were 267 cluster munitions casualties worldwide in 2006 (the majority in Lebanon).

Some would argue that a ban on cluster munitions is a luxury that we can afford in peacetime, but their absence would leave arsenals seriously deficient in war. Without cluster munitions massed rocket or artillery attacks would be used instead, which also leave explosive remnants that may harm civilians. A mid-course option would be a treaty to ensure that cluster munitions had reliable self-neutralizing mechanisms, thus retaining military utility whilst addressing humanitarian concerns.

Whilst the ICBL can claim to be a huge success, its concrete achievements are not easy to tease out of the tangle of rhetoric and statistics. To its detractors it has distorted the mines issue into a moral fashion. Not only has it failed to save a single life, it has distracted resources from mine clearance and perpetuated the problem, actually resulting in more lives being lost. To its supporters it is a triumph of a popular cause over a recalcitrant military industrial complex that has saved, and improved the quality of, thousands of lives and established a template that can be followed in pursuit of a ban on cluster munitions, then small arms, anti tank-mines and more. There will be many who hope they succeed in banning war before they might have cause to use any of these weapons.

Notes

1 The name 'Dumdum' comes from the town outside Calcutta in India where expanding bullets were manufactured for the British Indian Army. When smaller calibre bullets were introduced it was noticed that they did not have the same stopping power as the old-style, large lead balls, so a cross was scored across the tip of the bullet causing it to deform on contact with a body.

2 The other weapons were those with fragments that could not be detected by X-rays, blinding laser weapons and incendiary weapons such as napalm used against civilians.

3 The mandate given to the UN included aspects relating to human rights, the organization and conduct of free and fair general elections, military arrangements, civil administration, the maintenance of law and order, the repatriation and resettlement of the Cambodian refugees and displaced persons, and the rehabilitation of essential Cambodian infrastructure during the transitional period.

4 Known as Landmine Monitor (www.icbl.org/lm/). I used it as the primary source for figures throught this chapter.

Chapter 11

The End of the Mines?

—〰—

No exceptions, no reservations, no loopholes.
Jodie Williams, ICBL Coordinator

The fact that there are far fewer mines in the ground than originally estimated, the effects of the ICBL, the changing nature of war and the availability of more discriminating high-technology weapons combine to move us closer to a mine-free world than many appreciate. Firstly because there are not, and there never were, 110 million mines buried in the developing world. The original estimates produced by the UN were based on finger-in-the-air estimates, with the prevailing wind coming from a political rather than a practical direction. The figures were seized on by the ICBL and the media and became common currency, yet the more realistic estimates provided by deminers working in the field have consistently been met with an awkward silence or a mumbled statement about the numbers being unimportant. The humanitarian mine crisis of the late twentieth and early twenty-first centuries bears comparison with the post-Second World War situation. In 1945, rapid, large-scale, pragmatic action resulted in over 100 million mines being cleared in three years. In recent, more politicized times it has taken twenty years to clear 4 million mines. This leaves perhaps one million mines in the ground and these could be cleared, provided sufficient funding and appropriate prioritization, within a couple of years.

Prioritization is important as remaining minefields are often remote and have a limited impact on human development, so resources need to be concentrated on areas that will yield the greatest benefit to the largest number of people. Statistics on mine casualties have been collected for the past twenty years and are reasonably accurate. They have been expanded in recent years to include not only mine victims, but also victims of cluster munitions, other explosive remnants of war and victim-operated IEDs. The number of killed and injured by these various means has dropped from 20,000 annually in the early 1990s to 5,000 in 2006. To provide a degree of perspective, this is about the same number as those killed and injured worldwide annually by lightning. This is still too many deaths, and the casualty figures mask the impact of land made unavailable for development due to mines. It is practically impossible to clear all the remaining mines. Some mines will be found, sometimes with fatal consequences, many years from now. But dealing with the residual problems should be the work of small national teams, rather than international humanitarian efforts. With mounting evidence of degrading explosives in some of the most common types of Chinese and Soviet mines, the challenge may be to clear them before they lose their ability to function.

The ICBL did an extraordinary job in turning public opinion against mines. Millions of people around the world were sufficiently sickened by the grotesque and multifaceted effects of mines that two thirds of the world's countries signed the anti-personnel mine-ban treaty, resulting in the destruction of millions of stockpiled mines, and virtually eliminating the trade in mines. The countries that did not sign the ban have become acutely conscious of the damage to international reputations that the irresponsible use of mines could do. The stigma attached to mines, both anti-personnel and anti-tank, was the campaign's own 'force multiplier'. Non-signatories to the treaty have retained many millions of mines, but the threshold at which they might be used has risen considerably.

Some would argue that morality in war is a luxury that only those at peace can afford. The mine-ban treaty divides the world into those with a significant security threat and those who enjoy peace. There is a striking difference between the security profile of those leading the mine-ban treaty (Canada, Belgium and Switzerland) and those firmly amongst the non-signatories (US, Israel, Sri Lanka). Russia, a non-signatory to the mine-ban treaty, continues to use anti-personnel mines in Chechnya to protect vulnerable points because, according to the Chief of Russia's engineering troops, Colonel-General Nikolay Serdtsev, 'The Russian armed forces cannot allow themselves to give up the use of landmines, which for a long time will remain one of the most effective and inexpensive types of defensive weapon.' In some ways the mine-ban treaty can be considered a barometer of world peace. The momentum is in the right direction with 122 signatories in 1997 increasing to 155 signatories by 2008, while the number of mines laid since the treaty was first signed can be counted in the thousands.

The ICBL has certainly increased the threshold for laying mines, but it is important to recognize that at the same time the circumstances in which mines could be used has decreased. There are very few circumstances where states party to the mine-ban treaty would have used mines, even if their use was not banned or stigmatized. Mines were first used in large numbers as area-denial weapons to blunt armoured attacks in the Second World War. During the Cold War, to counter the threat of Soviet armoured attack, the use of massive minefields was central to the defence of the West, and mines developed into highly sophisticated scatterable systems with target-discriminating fuses, self-neutralization mechanisms and highly destructive warheads. The end of the Cold War eliminated one of the few credible scenarios in which massed armoured assaults might be launched and NATO tank numbers have halved since 1990. The last major anti-tank minefields laid were in Kuwait in 1991 and it is unlikely that similar types of minefield will be needed again.

In modern asymmetrical conflict (a large conventional army against a small guerrilla force) there are no circumstances in which conventional forces can use anti-tank mines. Guerrillas use civilian road vehicles and whilst modern mines can discriminate between a Russian and a US tank, they cannot distinguish between civilians and guerrillas in a Toyota. Whilst lack of target discrimination is one inhibitor, another is that guerrillas use public roads which would rarely be mined. In asymmetrical war there is a need for check points to regulate movements, but if lethal force is required at these, direct-fire weapons are much more effective, more discriminating and less likely to injure friendly troops.

Whilst conventional forces have no need of anti-tank mines in asymmetrical conflicts, anti-personnel mines might prove useful protecting isolated positions vulnerable to attack by guerrillas. To protect against this from guerrillas operating on foot, command-operated claymore-type mines remain legal, highly effective and do not constitute an undue risk to civilians after a war.

Whilst for conventional forces there are few scenarios when anti-tank or anti-personnel mines could be used, for guerrillas the situation is quite different and it is they who have laid most mines in the past ten years. And of course they have no legal status to sign the mine-ban treaty (but would not even if they could). Military vehicles have always been an ideal target for guerrillas – the asymmetry of a conflict can be defined by the image of a million-dollar tank destroyed by a ten-dollar mine. This form of attack has been the single most effective tactic used by guerrillas and insurgents in the past half a century, as deadly in Iraq in 2008 as it was in Vietnam in 1968. Whether the devices used in Iraq are mines or improvised explosive devices (IEDs) is a somewhat technical debate, but the tactical circumstances and the use of victim-operated roadside bombs make them very close relations.

Guerrillas also use anti-personnel mines to cause casualties amongst and to inhibit aggressive patrolling. The Colombian group FARC (Revolutionary Armed Forces of Colombia – Fuerzas Armadas Revolucionarias de Colombia) lays anti-personnel mines en masse and is currently one of the world's most prolific users. FARC uses mines principally to protect the drugs trade and they claimed over 1,000 casualties in 2006, which was by some way the highest concentration of casualties in the world. FARC is exceptional as most guerrillas lay anti-personnel mines, not to defend land, but to create fear and to inflict casualties. To achieve this, mines are laid individually or in small groups, more as booby traps than area-denial weapons.

The final factor taking us closer to a mine-free world is technology.

Successful combat in the Internet age demands an increasing sensitivity to host country, home country and international public opinion. Images of civilian suffering can rapidly change opinions and seriously undermine support for military operations. With TV cameras all over the modern battlefield, extreme care has to be taken to limit 'collateral damage'. The ideal is for modern war to be won, not by firepower, but by moral authority. As a banned or stigmatized weapon, the use of mines, with their inability to discriminate between civilians and combatants, risks undermining moral authority. New surveillance technology, however, changes this equation. Fit a mine with a surveillance system, a high-resolution digital camera, linked to a motion detector or heat sensor, with the images monitored remotely by a soldier who can fire a mine at will, and it ceases to become victim operated and therefore ceases to be a mine. The US is pioneering this so-called 'man-in-the-loop' technology. Their Spider 'networked munitions system' consists of eighty-four hand-emplaced explosive units with tripwires that signal the presence of an intruder to a controller who monitors the system centrally. Using infra-red camera or ground sensors, the controller can decide whether or not to fire any of the units.

The Spider is designed to be 'Ottawa compliant', controller rather than victim operated and easy to retrieve when no longer needed. But the ICBL is concerned that the system contains a battlefield override system which could take the man out of the loop leaving it to function as a victim-operated trap. The development of the Spider shows that the US, despite being a non-signatory to the mine-ban treaty, remains sensitive to the spirit of the treaty, yet determined that its defence posture should not be shaped by the disarmament lobby. But new surveillance technology means that mines can be as discriminating as most other weapons systems, and considerably more so than, say, artillery or long-range machine-gun fire.

In addition to man-in-the-loop mine systems, the increase in the number of aerial-surveillance platforms, especially unmanned systems, provide early warning and attack capabilities hitherto unimagined. They can act in many ways as area-denial weapons operating from the sky rather than buried in the ground, providing a range of tactical options for defenders. Surveillance systems can provide highly accurate targeting for artillery or air-delivered munitions, greatly increasing their effectiveness and further reducing the need for conventional minefields.

In various forms, mines have been a feature of war from the earliest of times. They are traditionally a defender's weapon, deployed in the face of an aggressor. As such they might have been considered positively. But they have never been consistently used responsibly and once buried they are remarkably difficult to recover. Uniquely, they do not recognize ceasefires and do not discern between soldiers and civilians.

A major consequence of the proliferation of plastic anti-personnel mines was tens of thousands of civilian casualties. It seems remarkable that these weapons could be used without an efficient means of clearing them once redundant. The good news is that mines have just about had their day; the bad news is that much of the suffering that they caused was preventable.

Appendix I

German Landmine Production
1939–45 (1,000s)

Anti-personnel Mines

Type	1939	1940	1941	1942	1943	1944	1945	Totals
Schrapnell mine 35	345	798	354	1,626	2,966	3,233	193	9,515
Schutzenmine 42	0	0	0	46	1,892	16,144	2,605	20,687
Stock mine 44	0	0	0	563	2,657	2,589	0	5,809
Glassmine 43	0	0	0	0	0	9,887	1,125	11,012
Fragmentation 4931	0	0	0	0	0	40	90	130
	345	798	354	2,235	7,515	31,893	4,013	47,153

Anti-tank Mines

Type	1939	1940	1941	1942	1943	1944	1945	Totals
Tellermine 35	188	502	605	2,180	743	0	0	4,218
Tellermine 35 steel	0	0	0	346	1,855	0	0	2,201
Tellermine 42	0	0	0	523	4,808	4,344	160	9,835
Tellermine 43	0	0	0	0	2,242	1,381	0	3,623
Light AT mine	0	0	23	9	0	0	0	32
Woodmine 42	0	0	0	1,535	2,450	1,317	0	5,302
Topfmine 4531	0	0	0	0	0	629	158	787
Riegelmine 43	0	0	0	0	0	25	2,886	2,911
Hollow-charge mine	0	0	0	0	0	30	29	59
Bottle mine	0	0	0	0	0	246	529	775
	188	502	628	4,593	12,098	7,972	3,762	29,743

Appendix 2

Table Showing Estimates of Mines Cleared in Various Countries and Casualties Sustained during Clearance Operations after the Second World War

Country	Period	Millions of Mines Cleared	Deminers Killed	Deminers Injured	Total Casualties	Mines Cleared per Casualty	Remarks
Austria	1945-75	0.046	18	23	41	1,122	
Belgium	1945-6	0.4	–	–	286	1,398	
Denmark	1945-7	0.75	190	250	440	1,704	
England	1944-57	0.35	155	55	210	1,666	
Finland	1945-76	0.066	–	–	–	–	No casualty data available
France	1945-8	13.0	2,127	3,630	5,757	2,258	
Germany	1945-7	0.76	108	113	221	3,439	Operation Tappet only
Guernsey	1945	0.067	8	14	22	4,786	
Holland	1945-6	1.08	205	407	613	1,762	
Italy	1945-6	3.0	–	–	1,100	2,727	
N. Africa	1943-90	est. 1.0	–	–	est. 600	1,667	Figures are very approximate
Norway	1945-47	0.75	192	275	467	1,606	
Poland	1945-56	14.76	404	571	975	15,138	Casualty figures extrapolated (and probably underestimated)
USSR	1945-6	58.5	–	–	29,000(-)	2,000	Casualty figures estimated
Totals	–	94.52	3,407	5,338	39,732	2,178	Mines Cleared per Casualty figure excludes Poland

Appendix 3

US FASCAM (Family of Scatterable Mines) Systems

Anti-personnel Mines

Name	Type of Mine	Delivery System	Mines per Canister
FLIPPER M74	Tripwire-initiated, fragmentation	Ground dispenser	Varies
MOPMS Modular Pack Mine System	Tripwire-initiated, fragmentation	Ground-emplaced	4
VOLCANO	Tripwire-initiated, fragmentation	Ground-projected or air-delivered	36
ADAM M67/M72 Area Denial ArtilleryMunition	Tripwire-initiated, bounding fragmentation	155mm artillery	5
GATOR BLU92B	Tripwire-initiated, bounding fragmentation	Air-delivered	22

Anti-tank Mines

Name	Type of Mine	Delivery System	Mines per Canister
FLIPPER M75	Shaped-charge warhead, magnetic-influence fuse	Ground-emplaced	5
MOPMS M76 Modular Pack Mine System	Shaped-charge warhead, magnetic-influence fuse	Ground-emplaced	17
VOLCANO	Shaped-charge warhead, magnetic-influence fuse	Ground-projected or air-delivered	6
RAAM M70 and M73 Remote Anti-Armor Mine	Shaped-charge warhead, magnetic-influence fuse	155mm Artillery	9
GATOR BLU91B	Shaped-charge warhead, magnetic-influence fuse	Air-delivered	72

Notes:
1. All FASCAM mines have self-destruct periods of four hours and five days.
2. A proportion of FASCAM mines are fitted with anti-handling devices.
3. Multiple canisters are usually deployed. For example, the Volcano ground-projected.

Convention on the Prohibition of the Use, Stockpiling, Production and Transfer of Anti-Personnel Mines and on their Destruction

—ᵐ—

Determined to put an end to the suffering and casualties caused by anti-personnel mines, that kill or maim hundreds of people every week, mostly innocent and defenceless civilians and especially children, obstruct economic development and reconstruction, inhibit the repatriation of refugees and internally displaced persons, and have other severe consequences for years after emplacement,

Believing it necessary to do their utmost to contribute in an efficient and coordinated manner to face the challenge of removing anti-personnel mines placed throughout the world, and to assure their destruction,

Wishing to do their utmost in providing assistance for the care and rehabilitation, including the social and economic reintegration of mine victims,

Recognizing that a total ban of anti-personnel mines would also be an important confidence-building measure,

Welcoming the adoption of the Protocol on Prohibitions or Restrictions on the Use of Mines, Booby-Traps and Other Devices, as amended on 3 May 1996, annexed to the Convention on Prohibitions or Restrictions on the Use of Certain Conventional Weapons Which May Be Deemed to Be Excessively Injurious or to

Have Indiscriminate Effects, and calling for the early ratification of this Protocol by all States which have not yet done so,

Welcoming also United Nations General Assembly Resolution 51/45 S of 10 December 1996 urging all States to pursue vigorously an effective, legally-binding international agreement to ban the use, stockpiling, production and transfer of anti-personnel landmines,

Welcoming furthermore the measures taken over the past years, both unilaterally and multilaterally, aiming at prohibiting, restricting or suspending the use, stockpiling, production and transfer of anti-personnel mines,

Stressing the role of public conscience in furthering the principles of humanity as evidenced by the call for a total ban of anti-personnel mines and recognizing the efforts to that end undertaken by the International Red Cross and Red Crescent Movement, the International Campaign to Ban Landmines and numerous other non-governmental organizations around the world,

Recalling the Ottawa Declaration of 5 October 1996 and the Brussels Declaration of 27 June 1997 urging the international community to negotiate an international and legally binding agreement prohibiting the use, stockpiling, production and transfer of anti-personnel mines,

Emphasizing the desirability of attracting the adherence of all States to this Convention, and determined to work strenuously towards the promotion of its universalization in all relevant fora including, inter alia, the United Nations, the Conference on Disarmament, regional organizations, and groupings, and review conferences of the Convention on Prohibitions or Restrictions on the Use of Certain Conventional Weapons Which May Be Deemed to Be Excessively Injurious or to Have Indiscriminate Effects,

Basing themselves on the principle of international humanitarian law that the right of the parties to an armed conflict to choose methods or means of warfare is not unlimited, on the principle that prohibits the employment in armed conflicts of weapons, projectiles and materials and methods of warfare of a nature to cause superfluous injury or unnecessary suffering and on the principle that a distinction must be made between civilians and combatants,

Have agreed as follows:

Article 1
General obligations

1. Each State Party undertakes never under any circumstances:
a) To use anti-personnel mines;
b) To develop, produce, otherwise acquire, stockpile, retain or transfer to anyone, directly or indirectly, anti-personnel mines;
c) To assist, encourage or induce, in any way, anyone to engage in any activity prohibited to a State Party under this Convention.
2. Each State Party undertakes to destroy or ensure the destruction of all anti-personnel mines in accordance with the provisions of this Convention.

Article 2
Definitions

1. 'Anti-personnel mine' means a mine designed to be exploded by the presence, proximity or contact of a person and that will incapacitate, injure or kill one or more persons. Mines designed to be detonated by the presence, proximity or contact of a vehicle as opposed to a person, that are equipped with anti-handling devices, are not considered anti-personnel mines as a result of being so equipped.
2. 'Mine' means a munition designed to be placed under, on or near the ground or other surface area and to be exploded by the presence, proximity or contact of a person or a vehicle.
3. 'Anti-handling device' means a device intended to protect a mine and which is part of, linked to, attached to or placed under the mine and which activates when an attempt is made to tamper with or otherwise intentionally disturb the mine.

4. 'Transfer' involves, in addition to the physical movement of anti-personnel mines into or from national territory, the transfer of title to and control over the mines, but does not involve the transfer of territory containing emplaced anti-personnel mines.

5. 'Mined area' means an area which is dangerous due to the presence or suspected presence of mines.

Article 3
Exceptions

1. Notwithstanding the general obligations under Article 1, the retention or transfer of a number of anti-personnel mines for the development of and training in mine detection, mine clearance, or mine destruction techniques is permitted. The amount of such mines shall not exceed the minimum number absolutely necessary for the above-mentioned purposes.

2. The transfer of anti-personnel mines for the purpose of destruction is permitted.

Article 4
Destruction of stockpiled anti-personnel mines

Except as provided for in Article 3, each State Party undertakes to destroy or ensure the destruction of all stockpiled anti-personnel mines it owns or possesses, or that are under its jurisdiction or control, as soon as possible but not later than four years after the entry into force of this Convention for that State Party.

Article 5
Destruction of anti-personnel mines in mined areas

1. Each State Party undertakes to destroy or ensure the destruction of all anti-personnel mines in mined areas under its jurisdiction or control, as soon as possible but not later than ten years after the entry into force of this Convention for that State Party.

2. Each State Party shall make every effort to identify all areas under its jurisdiction or control in which anti-personnel mines are known or

suspected to be emplaced and shall ensure as soon as possible that all anti-personnel mines in mined areas under its jurisdiction or control are perimeter-marked, monitored and protected by fencing or other means, to ensure the effective exclusion of civilians, until all anti-personnel mines contained therein have been destroyed. The marking shall at least be to the standards set out in the Protocol on Prohibitions or Restrictions on the Use of Mines, Booby-Traps and Other Devices, as amended on 3 May 1996, annexed to the Convention on Prohibitions or Restrictions on the Use of Certain Conventional Weapons Which May Be Deemed to Be Excessively Injurious or to Have Indiscriminate Effects.

3. If a State Party believes that it will be unable to destroy or ensure the destruction of all anti-personnel mines referred to in paragraph 1 within that time period, it may submit a request to a Meeting of the States Parties or a Review Conference for an extension of the deadline for completing the destruction of such anti-personnel mines, for a period of up to ten years.

4. Each request shall contain:

a) The duration of the proposed extension;

b) A detailed explanation of the reasons for the proposed extension, including:

(i) The preparation and status of work conducted under national demining programs;

(ii) The financial and technical means available to the State Party for the destruction of all the anti-personnel mines; and

(iii) Circumstances which impede the ability of the State Party to destroy all the anti-personnel mines in mined areas;

c) The humanitarian, social, economic, and environmental implications of the extension; and

d) Any other information relevant to the request for the proposed extension.

5. The Meeting of the States Parties or the Review Conference shall, taking into consideration the factors contained in paragraph 4, assess the request and decide by a majority of votes of States Parties present and voting whether to grant the request for an extension period.

6. Such an extension may be renewed upon the submission of a new request in accordance with paragraphs 3, 4 and 5 of this Article. In

requesting a further extension period a State Party shall submit relevant additional information on what has been undertaken in the previous extension period pursuant to this Article.

Article 6
International cooperation and assistance

1. In fulfilling its obligations under this Convention each State Party has the right to seek and receive assistance, where feasible, from other States Parties to the extent possible.
2. Each State Party undertakes to facilitate and shall have the right to participate in the fullest possible exchange of equipment, material and scientific and technological information concerning the implementation of this Convention. The States Parties shall not impose undue restrictions on the provision of mine clearance equipment and related technological information for humanitarian purposes.
3. Each State Party in a position to do so shall provide assistance for the care and rehabilitation, and social and economic reintegration, of mine victims and for mine awareness programs. Such assistance may be provided, inter alia, through the United Nations system, international, regional or national organizations or institutions, the International Committee of the Red Cross, national Red Cross and Red Crescent societies and their International Federation, non-governmental organizations, or on a bilateral basis.
4. Each State Party in a position to do so shall provide assistance for mine clearance and related activities. Such assistance may be provided, inter alia, through the United Nations system, international or regional organizations or institutions, non-governmental organizations or institutions, or on a bilateral basis, or by contributing to the United Nations Voluntary Trust Fund for Assistance in Mine Clearance, or other regional funds that deal with demining.
5. Each State Party in a position to do so shall provide assistance for the destruction of stockpiled anti-personnel mines.
6. Each State Party undertakes to provide information to the database

on mine clearance established within the United Nations system, especially information concerning various means and technologies of mine clearance, and lists of experts, expert agencies or national points of contact on mine clearance.

7. States Parties may request the United Nations, regional organizations, other States Parties or other competent intergovernmental or non-governmental fora to assist its authorities in the elaboration of a national demining program to determine, inter alia:

a) The extent and scope of the anti-personnel mine problem;

b) The financial, technological and human resources that are required for the implementation of the program;

c) The estimated number of years necessary to destroy all anti-personnel mines in mined areas under the jurisdiction or control of the concerned State Party;

d) Mine awareness activities to reduce the incidence of mine-related injuries or deaths;

e) Assistance to mine victims;

f) The relationship between the Government of the concerned State Party and the relevant governmental, inter-governmental or non-governmental entities that will work in the implementation of the program.

8. Each State Party giving and receiving assistance under the provisions of this Article shall cooperate with a view to ensuring the full and prompt implementation of agreed assistance programs.

Article 7
Transparency measures

1. Each State Party shall report to the Secretary-General of the United Nations as soon as practicable, and in any event not later than 180 days after the entry into force of this Convention for that State Party on:

a) The national implementation measures referred to in Article 9;

b) The total of all stockpiled anti-personnel mines owned or possessed by it, or under its jurisdiction or control, to include a breakdown of the type, quantity and, if possible, lot numbers of each type of anti-personnel mine stockpiled;

c) To the extent possible, the location of all mined areas that contain, or are suspected to contain, anti-personnel mines under its jurisdiction or control, to include as much detail as possible regarding the type and quantity of each type of anti-personnel mine in each mined area and when they were emplaced;

d) The types, quantities and, if possible, lot numbers of all anti-personnel mines retained or transferred for the development of and training in mine detection, mine clearance or mine destruction techniques, or transferred for the purpose of destruction, as well as the institutions authorized by a State Party to retain or transfer anti-personnel mines, in accordance with Article 3;

e) The status of programs for the conversion or de-commissioning of anti-personnel mine production facilities;

f) The status of programs for the destruction of anti-personnel mines in accordance with Articles 4 and 5, including details of the methods which will be used in destruction, the location of all destruction sites and the applicable safety and environmental standards to be observed;

g) The types and quantities of all anti-personnel mines destroyed after the entry into force of this Convention for that State Party, to include a breakdown of the quantity of each type of anti-personnel mine destroyed, in accordance with Articles 4 and 5, respectively, along with, if possible, the lot numbers of each type of anti-personnel mine in the case of destruction in accordance with Article 4;

h) The technical characteristics of each type of anti-personnel mine produced, to the extent known, and those currently owned or possessed by a State Party, giving, where reasonably possible, such categories of information as may facilitate identification and clearance of anti-personnel mines; at a minimum, this information shall include the dimensions, fusing, explosive content, metallic content, colour photographs and other information which may facilitate mine clearance; and

i) The measures taken to provide an immediate and effective warning to the population in relation to all areas identified under paragraph 2 of Article 5.

2. The information provided in accordance with this Article shall be updated by the States Parties annually, covering the last calendar year,

and reported to the Secretary-General of the United Nations not later than 30 April of each year.

3. The Secretary-General of the United Nations shall transmit all such reports received to the States Parties.

Article 8
Facilitation and clarification of compliance

1. The States Parties agree to consult and cooperate with each other regarding the implementation of the provisions of this Convention, and to work together in a spirit of cooperation to facilitate compliance by States Parties with their obligations under this Convention.

2. If one or more States Parties wish to clarify and seek to resolve questions relating to compliance with the provisions of this Convention by another State Party, it may submit, through the Secretary-General of the United Nations, a Request for Clarification of that matter to that State Party. Such a request shall be accompanied by all appropriate information. Each State Party shall refrain from unfounded Requests for Clarification, care being taken to avoid abuse. A State Party that receives a Request for Clarification shall provide, through the Secretary-General of the United Nations, within 28 days to the requesting State Party all information which would assist in clarifying this matter.

3. If the requesting State Party does not receive a response through the Secretary-General of the United Nations within that time period, or deems the response to the Request for Clarification to be unsatisfactory, it may submit the matter through the Secretary-General of the United Nations to the next Meeting of the States Parties. The Secretary-General of the United Nations shall transmit the submission, accompanied by all appropriate information pertaining to the Request for Clarification, to all States Parties. All such information shall be presented to the requested State Party which shall have the right to respond.

4. Pending the convening of any meeting of the States Parties, any of the States Parties concerned may request the Secretary-General of the United Nations to exercise his or her good offices to facilitate the clarification requested.

5. The requesting State Party may propose through the Secretary-General of the United Nations the convening of a Special Meeting of the States Parties to consider the matter. The Secretary-General of the United Nations shall thereupon communicate this proposal and all information submitted by the States Parties concerned, to all States Parties with a request that they indicate whether they favour a Special Meeting of the States Parties, for the purpose of considering the matter. In the event that within 14 days from the date of such communication, at least one-third of the States Parties favours such a Special Meeting, the Secretary-General of the United Nations shall convene this Special Meeting of the States Parties within a further 14 days. A quorum for this Meeting shall consist of a majority of States Parties.

6. The Meeting of the States Parties or the Special Meeting of the States Parties, as the case may be, shall first determine whether to consider the matter further, taking into account all information submitted by the States Parties concerned. The Meeting of the States Parties or the Special Meeting of the States Parties shall make every effort to reach a decision by consensus. If despite all efforts to that end no agreement has been reached, it shall take this decision by a majority of States Parties present and voting.

7. All States Parties shall cooperate fully with the Meeting of the States Parties or the Special Meeting of the States Parties in the fulfilment of its review of the matter, including any fact-finding missions that are authorized in accordance with paragraph 8.

8. If further clarification is required, the Meeting of the States Parties or the Special Meeting of the States Parties shall authorize a fact-finding mission and decide on its mandate by a majority of States Parties present and voting. At any time the requested State Party may invite a fact-finding mission to its territory. Such a mission shall take place without a decision by a Meeting of the States Parties or a Special Meeting of the States Parties to authorize such a mission. The mission, consisting of up to 9 experts, designated and approved in accordance with paragraphs 9 and 10, may collect additional information on the spot or in other places directly related to the alleged compliance issue under the jurisdiction or control of the requested State Party.

9. The Secretary-General of the United Nations shall prepare and update a list of the names, nationalities and other relevant data of qualified experts provided by States Parties and communicate it to all States Parties. Any expert included on this list shall be regarded as designated for all fact-finding missions unless a State Party declares its non-acceptance in writing. In the event of non-acceptance, the expert shall not participate in fact-finding missions on the territory or any other place under the jurisdiction or control of the objecting State Party, if the non-acceptance was declared prior to the appointment of the expert to such missions.

10. Upon receiving a request from the Meeting of the States Parties or a Special Meeting of the States Parties, the Secretary-General of the United Nations shall, after consultations with the requested State Party, appoint the members of the mission, including its leader. Nationals of States Parties requesting the fact-finding mission or directly affected by it shall not be appointed to the mission. The members of the fact-finding mission shall enjoy privileges and immunities under Article VI of the Convention on the Privileges and Immunities of the United Nations, adopted on 13 February 1946.

11. Upon at least 72 hours notice, the members of the fact-finding mission shall arrive in the territory of the requested State Party at the earliest opportunity. The requested State Party shall take the necessary administrative measures to receive, transport and accommodate the mission, and shall be responsible for ensuring the security of the mission to the maximum extent possible while they are on territory under its control.

12. Without prejudice to the sovereignty of the requested State Party, the fact-finding mission may bring into the territory of the requested State Party the necessary equipment which shall be used exclusively for gathering information on the alleged compliance issue. Prior to its arrival, the mission will advise the requested State Party of the equipment that it intends to utilize in the course of its fact-finding mission.

13. The requested State Party shall make all efforts to ensure that the fact-finding mission is given the opportunity to speak with all relevant persons who may be able to provide information related to the alleged compliance issue.

14. The requested State Party shall grant access for the fact-finding mission to all areas and installations under its control where facts relevant to the compliance issue could be expected to be collected. This shall be subject to any arrangements that the requested State Party considers necessary for:

a) The protection of sensitive equipment, information and areas;

b) The protection of any constitutional obligations the requested State Party may have with regard to proprietary rights, searches and seizures, or other constitutional rights; or

c) The physical protection and safety of the members of the fact-finding mission.

In the event that the requested State Party makes such arrangements, it shall make every reasonable effort to demonstrate through alternative means its compliance with this Convention.

15. The fact-finding mission may remain in the territory of the State Party concerned for no more than 14 days, and at any particular site no more than 7 days, unless otherwise agreed.

16. All information provided in confidence and not related to the subject matter of the fact-finding mission shall be treated on a confidential basis.

17. The fact-finding mission shall report, through the Secretary-General of the United Nations, to the Meeting of the States Parties or the Special Meeting of the States Parties the results of its findings.

18. The Meeting of the States Parties or the Special Meeting of the States Parties shall consider all relevant information, including the report submitted by the fact-finding mission, and may request the requested State Party to take measures to address the compliance issue within a specified period of time. The requested State Party shall report on all measures taken in response to this request.

19. The Meeting of the States Parties or the Special Meeting of the States Parties may suggest to the States Parties concerned ways and means to further clarify or resolve the matter under consideration, including the initiation of appropriate procedures in conformity with international law. In circumstances where the issue at hand is determined to be due to circumstances beyond the control of the requested State Party, the Meeting of the States Parties or the Special

Meeting of the States Parties may recommend appropriate measures, including the use of cooperative measures referred to in Article 6.

20. The Meeting of the States Parties or the Special Meeting of the States Parties shall make every effort to reach its decisions referred to in paragraphs 18 and 19 by consensus, otherwise by a two-thirds majority of States Parties present and voting.

Article 9
National implementation measures

Each State Party shall take all appropriate legal, administrative and other measures, including the imposition of penal sanctions, to prevent and suppress any activity prohibited to a State Party under this Convention undertaken by persons or on territory under its jurisdiction or control.

Article 10
Settlement of disputes

1. The States Parties shall consult and cooperate with each other to settle any dispute that may arise with regard to the application or the interpretation of this Convention. Each State Party may bring any such dispute before the Meeting of the States Parties.

2. The Meeting of the States Parties may contribute to the settlement of the dispute by whatever means it deems appropriate, including offering its good offices, calling upon the States parties to a dispute to start the settlement procedure of their choice and recommending a time-limit for any agreed procedure.

3. This Article is without prejudice to the provisions of this Convention on facilitation and clarification of compliance.

Article 11
Meetings of the States Parties

1. The States Parties shall meet regularly in order to consider any matter with regard to the application or implementation of this Convention, including:

a) The operation and status of this Convention;

b) Matters arising from the reports submitted under the provisions of this Convention;

c) International cooperation and assistance in accordance with Article 6;

d) The development of technologies to clear anti-personnel mines;

e) Submissions of States Parties under Article 8; and

f) Decisions relating to submissions of States Parties as provided for in Article 5.

2. The First Meeting of the States Parties shall be convened by the Secretary-General of the United Nations within one year after the entry into force of this Convention. The subsequent meetings shall be convened by the Secretary-General of the United Nations annually until the first Review Conference.

3. Under the conditions set out in Article 8, the Secretary-General of the United Nations shall convene a Special Meeting of the States Parties.

4. States not parties to this Convention, as well as the United Nations, other relevant international organizations or institutions, regional organizations, the International Committee of the Red Cross and relevant non-governmental organizations may be invited to attend these meetings as observers in accordance with the agreed Rules of Procedure.

Article 12
Review Conferences

1. A Review Conference shall be convened by the Secretary-General of the United Nations five years after the entry into force of this Convention. Further Review Conferences shall be convened by the Secretary-General of the United Nations if so requested by one or more States Parties, provided that the interval between Review Conferences shall in no case be less than five years. All States Parties to this Convention shall be invited to each Review Conference.

2. The purpose of the Review Conference shall be:

a) To review the operation and status of this Convention;

b) To consider the need for and the interval between further Meetings of the States Parties referred to in paragraph 2 of Article 11;

c) To take decisions on submissions of States Parties as provided for in Article 5; and

d) To adopt, if necessary, in its final report conclusions related to the implementation of this Convention.

3. States not parties to this Convention, as well as the United Nations, other relevant international organizations or institutions, regional organizations, the International Committee of the Red Cross and relevant non-governmental organizations may be invited to attend each Review Conference as observers in accordance with the agreed Rules of Procedure.

Article 13
Amendments

1. At any time after the entry into force of this Convention any State Party may propose amendments to this Convention. Any proposal for an amendment shall be communicated to the Depositary, who shall circulate it to all States Parties and shall seek their views on whether an Amendment Conference should be convened to consider the proposal. If a majority of the States Parties notify the Depositary no later than 30 days after its circulation that they support further consideration of the proposal, the Depositary shall convene an Amendment Conference to which all States Parties shall be invited.

2. States not parties to this Convention, as well as the United Nations, other relevant international organizations or institutions, regional organizations, the International Committee of the Red Cross and relevant non-governmental organizations may be invited to attend each Amendment Conference as observers in accordance with the agreed Rules of Procedure.

3. The Amendment Conference shall be held immediately following a Meeting of the States Parties or a Review Conference unless a majority of the States Parties request that it be held earlier.

4. Any amendment to this Convention shall be adopted by a majority of two-thirds of the States Parties present and voting at the Amendment Conference. The Depositary shall communicate any amendment so adopted to the States Parties.

5. An amendment to this Convention shall enter into force for all States Parties to this Convention which have accepted it, upon the deposit with the Depositary of instruments of acceptance by a majority of States Parties. Thereafter it shall enter into force for any remaining State Party on the date of deposit of its instrument of acceptance.

Article 14
Costs

1. The costs of the Meetings of the States Parties, the Special Meetings of the States Parties, the Review Conferences and the Amendment Conferences shall be borne by the States Parties and States not parties to this Convention participating therein, in accordance with the United Nations scale of assessment adjusted appropriately.
2. The costs incurred by the Secretary-General of the United Nations under Articles 7 and 8 and the costs of any fact-finding mission shall be borne by the States Parties in accordance with the United Nations scale of assessment adjusted appropriately.

Article 15
Signature
This Convention, done at Oslo, Norway, on 18 September 1997, shall be open for signature at Ottawa, Canada, by all States from 3 December 1997 until 4 December 1997, and at the United Nations Headquarters in New York from 5 December 1997 until its entry into force.

Article 16
Ratification, acceptance, approval or accession
1. This Convention is subject to ratification, acceptance or approval of the Signatories.
2. It shall be open for accession by any State which has not signed the Convention.
3. The instruments of ratification, acceptance, approval or accession shall be deposited with the Depositary.

Article 17
Entry into force

1. This Convention shall enter into force on the first day of the sixth month after the month in which the 40th instrument of ratification, acceptance, approval or accession has been deposited.
2. For any State which deposits its instrument of ratification, acceptance, approval or accession after the date of the deposit of the 40th instrument of ratification, acceptance, approval or accession, this Convention shall enter into force on the first day of the sixth month after the date on which that State has deposited its instrument of ratification, acceptance, approval or accession.

Article 18
Provisional application

Any State may at the time of its ratification, acceptance, approval or accession, declare that it will apply provisionally paragraph 1 of Article 1 of this Convention pending its entry into force.

Article 19
Reservations
The Articles of this Convention shall not be subject to reservations.

Article 20
Duration and withdrawal

1. This Convention shall be of unlimited duration.
2. Each State Party shall, in exercising its national sovereignty, have the right to withdraw from this Convention. It shall give notice of such withdrawal to all other States Parties, to the Depositary and to the United Nations Security Council. Such instrument of withdrawal shall include a full explanation of the reasons motivating this withdrawal.
3. Such withdrawal shall only take effect six months after the receipt of the instrument of withdrawal by the Depositary. If, however, on

the expiry of that six- month period, the withdrawing State Party is engaged in an armed conflict, the withdrawal shall not take effect before the end of the armed conflict.

4. The withdrawal of a State Party from this Convention shall not in any way affect the duty of States to continue fulfilling the obligations assumed under any relevant rules of international law.

Article 21
Depositary

The Secretary-General of the United Nations is hereby designated as the Depositary of this Convention.

Article 22
Authentic texts

The original of this Convention, of which the Arabic, Chinese, English, French, Russian and Spanish texts are equally authentic, shall be deposited with the Secretary-General of the United Nations.

Select Bibliography

—⚏—

Books

Ambrose, Stephen, E., *D-Day June 6, 1944: The Climactic Battle of World War II*, New York, Simon and Schuster, 1994.

The Arms Project of Human Rights Watch, *Landmines: A Deadly Legacy*, New York, HRW and PHR, 1993.

Beck, Alfred M. et al., *US Army in WW2, The Technical Services: The Corps of Engineers: The War against Germany*, Washington DC, Centre for Military History, 1985.

Bishop, M.C. and Coulston J.C.N., *Roman Military Equipment*, London, Batsford, 1993.

Bottigliero, Ilaria, *120 Million landmines Deployed Worldwide: Fact or Fiction?* Barnsley, Leo Cooper 2000.

Brown, G.I., *The Big Bang: A History of Explosives*, Stroud, Sutton Publishing, 1998.

Caesar, J., *The Conquest of Gaul*, London: Penguin, 1951.

——, *Commentaries on the Gallic War*, trans. S.A. Handford, Penguin, 1951.

Coll, B.D., Keith, J.E. and Rosenthal, H.H, *The Corps of Engineers: Troops and Equipment*, Washington DC, Department of the Army, 1968.

Cordesman, Anthony H. and Wagner Abraham R., *The Lessons of Modern Warfare*, vol. 1, The Arab Israeli Conflicts 1973-89, Boulder, Westview Press, 1990.

——, *The Lessons of Modern Warfare*, vol. IV, *The Gulf War*, Boulder, Westview Press, 1996.

Croll, M., *The History of Landmines*, Leo Cooper, 1998.

Davis, R.H.C., *The Medieval Warhorse: Origin, Development and Redevelopment*, London, Thames and Hudson, 1989.

Davies, Paul and Dunlop, Nick, *War of the Mines: Cambodia and the Impoverishment of a Nation*, London, Pluto Press, 1994.

Doubler, Michael D., *Closing with the Enemy: How GIs Fought the War in Europe 1944-45*, Kansas, Kansas University Press, 1994.

Farwell, Byron, *The Great War in Africa*, London, W. Norton & Company, 1986.

Ffoulkes, C., *Arms and Armaments: A Historical Survey of Weapons of the British Army*, London, George Harrap and Company Ltd., 1945.

Gardner, Brian, *The German East*, London: Cassel, 1963.

Gilbert, Felix, *Hitler Directs His War: The Secret Records of his Daily Military Conferences*, New York, Oxford University Press, 1950.

Hamilton, Nigel, Monty: *The Making of a General 1887-1942*, London, McGraw-Hill Book Company, 1981.

Hartcup, Guy, *The Challenge of War: Britain's Scientific and Engineering Contributions to World War Two,* New York, Taplinger Publishing Company, 1970.

Hartley A.B., *Unexploded Bomb: The Story of Bomb Disposal,* New York, W.W. Norton & Company, 1958.

Hay Jr., Lieutenant General John H., *Vietnam Studies: Tactical and Material Innovations,* Washington DC, Department of the Army, 1974.

Heyman, Major Charles, *Trends in Landmine Warfare,* Coulsdon, Jane's Information Group, August 1995.

Hogben, Major Arthur, *Designed to Kill,* Wellingborough, Patrick Stephens, 1987.

Hoppen, Alison, *The Fortification of Malta by the Order of St John,* Edinburgh, Scottish Academic Press, 1979.

Jefferson, Paul, *Warsaw Pact Mines,* Basildon, Miltra Engineering, 1992.

Jones, Ian, *Malice Afterthought: A History of Booby Traps from WW1 to Vietnam,* Stackpole Books, 2005.

Keegan, John, *A History of Warfare,* New York, Vintage Books, 1993.

King, Colin (ed.), *Jane's Mines and Mine Clearance 2004 – 2005,* Jane's, 2004.

Liddell Hart, B.H., *The Tanks, vol. 2,* London, Cassel and Company, 1959.

Liddell Hart, B.H. (ed.), *The Red Army,* New York, Harcourt, Brace and Co., 1956.

Majdalany, Fred, *The Battle of El Alemein,* New York, J.B. Lippencot and Company, 1964.

Maslen, Stuart, *Mine Action after Diana: Progress in the Struggle against Landmines,* Pluto Press 2004.

Mayo, Linda, US Army in WW2, *The Technical Services: The Ordnance Department on Beachhead and Battlefront,* Washington DC, Office of the Chief of Military History, 1968.

McDonald, Charles B., *US Army in WW2, European Theatre of Operations: The Siegfried Line Campaign,* Washington DC, Department of the Army, 1963.

McLaughlin-Green, Constance, Thompson, Harry C. and Roots, Peter C., *US Army in WW2: The Technical Services: The Ordnance Department: Planning Munitions for War,* Washington DC, Office of the Chief of Military History, Department of the Army, 1955.

Pakenham-Walsh, Major General R.P., *The History of the Corps of Royal Engineers,* vols VIII to X, Chatham, Institute of Royal Engineers vol. VIII 1958, vol. X 1986.

Perry, Milton F, *Infernal Machines: The Story of Confederate Submarine and Mine Warfare,* Baton Rouge, Louisiana State University Press, 1985 (first published 1965).

Roberts, Shawn and Williams, Jody, *After the Guns Fall Silent: The Enduring Legacy of Landmines,* Washington DC, Vietnam Veterans of America Foundation, 1995.

Sloane, RE, Lieutenant Colonel C.E.E., *Mine Warfare on Land,* London, Brassey's, 1986.

Starry, Donn A., *Mounted Combat in Vietnam,* Washington DC, Department of the Army 1977.

Stiff, Peter, *Taming the Landmine,* Alberton, Galago, 1986.

United States Department of State, *Hidden Killers: The Global Landmine Crisis,* Washington DC, 1994.

Veasy-Fitzgerald, Brian, *The Book of the Dog,* Los Angeles, Bordon, 1948.

Voldman, Danielle, *Attention Mines 1944-47*, Paris, France-Empire, 1985 (in French).

Westing, Arthur H., *Explosive Remnants of War*, London, Taylor and Francis, 1985.

Articles

Beckingham, Capt. H.W., 'Minefield Clearance in Guernsey', *The Royal Engineers Journal*, vol. 107, No. 2, August 1993.

Crothswaite, Major M.L., 'Demolitions and Minelaying, some German Methods', *The Royal Engineers Journal*, vol. LXVI, March–December 1952.

Dewing, Captain R.H., 'Anti-tank Mines in Mobile Warfare, *The Royal Engineers Journal*, March 1924.

Fitzpatrick, Lieutenant Colonel N.T., 'An Anti-Tank Exercise (Southern Command 1934)', *The Royal Engineers Journal*, vol.XLIX, March–December 1935.

Halloran, Bernard F., 'Soviet Landmine Warfare', *The Military Engineer*, March–April 1972, vol. 64, No. 418.

Hogben, Major Arthur, 'Background Notes on the Butterfly Bomb Attacks', *The Royal Engineers Journal*, vol. 107, No. 2, August 1993.

Hough Captain R.H., 'Disposal of Old Minefields in the United Kingdom', *The Royal Engineers Journal*, vol. LXVIII, No. 3, September 1954.

Lambert, Colonel J.M., 'Tin Triangles', *The Royal Engineers Journal,* vol. LXVI, March–December 1952.

Moore, Brigadier P.N.M., 'Mine Clearance – El Alamein, *The Royal Engineers Journal*, vol. 106, No. 3, December 1992.

Schneck, William, 'The Origins of Military Mines', *Engineer Bulletin*, July 1998.

Smith, Dr Chris (ed.), 'The Military Utility of Landmines', Centre for Defence Studies, King's College, June 1996.

Young, Brigadier B.K., 'The Development of Landmine Warfare, *The Army Quarterly*, January 1945, vol. XLIX, No. 2, pp. 189-99.

Youngblood, Norman Edgar, 'The Development of Landmine Warfare', Doctoral Thesis, Lubbock, TX, Texas Technical University, 2002.

Military References

Donovan P.D. and Moat R.D., RARDE Memorandum 38/83, 'History of Mines in Landwarfare', Fort Halstead, Kent, June 1983.

General Staff, 'Hints of Reconnaissance for Mines and Landmines in the Area Evacuated by the Germans', May 1917.

HQ 2nd British Infantry Division, Report on Operation Tappet, 'Mineclearance in 2 Div. and 1 Belgian Corps Area 15 Nov 1946–28 July 1947', BAOR, August 1947.

'Interim Instruction on the Nuclear Mine (Blue Peacock) 1955' (Secret – declassified), National Archive, AVIA 65/2065.

Military Operational Research Unit, 'Report No. 7, Minefield Clearance and Casualties', 3 May 1946.

Royal Engineers, 'Bomb Disposal – Historical Notes 1948–78'.

Royal Engineers Planning Staff, 'The Requirement for AT mines in the period 1965–75' (Secret – declassified), 1960.

School of Military Engineering, 'The Work of the Royal Engineers in the

European War 1914-19', Chatham, SME, 1924.

School of Military Engineering, 'Fortification Circular No. 57, German Traps and Mines', Chatham: SME, 1919.

Supreme Headquarters Allied Forces Europe, '1945 Employment of Enemy PoWs to clear Minefields', National Archieve, WO 229/7/22.

Technical History No. XXll, 'Landmine Clearance, Project 65 Hedgerow', National Archive, ADM277/21.

War Department Report 860, 'Aerial Bombardment of Minefields', 30 August 1944.

War Department, Technical Manual TM-E-30451, 'Handbook on German Military Forces', Washington DC, 1945.

War Office, 'Illustrated Record of German Army Equipment', vol. V, 'Mines, Mine Detectors and Demolition Equipment', London, 1947.

War Office, Military Engineering, Part 1, 'Field Defences', Chatham, SME, 1902.

War Office, 'Illustrated Record of German Army Equipment 1939-45', vol. V, 'Mines, Mine Detectors and Demolition Equipment', 1947.

Engineer Agency for Resource Inventories, Washington DC, 'Landmine and Countermine Warfare', June 1972:

'Environmental Assists and Constraints, Europe'

'Eastern Europe'

'Western Europe'

'North Africa 1940–43'

'Italy 1943–44'

'Korea 1950–54'

'Vietnam 64–69'

Websites

http://www.icbl.org – International Campaign to Ban Landmines.

http://tewton.narod.ru/mines – Russian Mines.

http://www.geocities.com/Augusta/8172/panzerfaust11.htm – German Mines.

http://www.lexikon-der-wehrmacht.de/ – German Military Equipment.

http://www.mineaction.org/ – United Nations Electronic Mine Information Network.

http://www.gichd.org/ – Geneva International Centre for Humanitarian Demining.

http://www.icrc.org/Eng/mines – International Committee of the Red Cross, Landmines and Explosive Remnants of War.

http://maic.jmu – James Madison University, Mine Action Information Centre.

Index

—ᨠᨠ—